ENGLISH

ISEB Revision Guide

Susan Elkin

www.galorepark.co.uk

Published by ISEB Publications, an imprint of Galore Park Publications Ltd
19/21 Sayers Lane, Tenterden, Kent TN30 6BW
www.galorepark.co.uk

Design and typesetting Typetechnique

Printed by Replika Press, India

ISBN-13: 978 0 903627 57 3

First published 2008, reprinted 2008, 2009

Details of other ISEB Revision Guides for Common Entrance, examination papers and Galore Park publications are available at www.galorepark.co.uk

The publishers are grateful for permission to use the extracts as follows: Extract from The Swan Kingdom by Zoë Marriot. Text © 2007 Zoë Marriot. Reproduced by Permission of Walker Books Ltd, London SE11 5HJ; extract from The Young Oxford Encyclopedia of Science (OUP, 2001), reprinted by permission of the publisher, Oxford University Press; 'Sunken Evening' by Laurie Lee, reprinted by permission of PFD on behalf of the Estate of Laurie Lee © Laurie Lee 1983; extract from 'Table Talk' by A. A. Gill, Sunday Times, 22 July 2007, © A. A. Gill, NI Syndication Limited, 2007, reproduced with permission. Front cover photo: Andrew Fox/Alamy.

About the author

Susan Elkin M.A., B.A. (Hons.), Cert. Ed. taught English for 36 years and was a member of the English department at Benenden from 1993 to 2004. She is now a full-time freelance writer and journalist and is author of *So you really want to learn English* Books 1, 2 and 3, published by Galore Park.

Contents

Introduction ... vi

Chapter 1: Comprehension and reading ... 1

1.1 How to approach a fiction or non-fiction comprehension passage ... 1

1.2 Different types of writing ... 2

Chapter 2: Reading at 11+ ... 10

2.1 11+ Comprehension exercise on a fiction passage ... 10

2.2 11+ Comprehension exercise on a non-fiction passage ... 13

Chapter 3: Reading at 13+ (non-fiction) ... 17

3.1 13+ Exercise on a non-fiction text ... 17

Chapter 4: Reading at 13+ (poetry) ... 21

4.1 Revising the 'tools' of poetry ... 21

4.2 Comprehension exercise on a poem ... 24

Chapter 5: Reading at scholarship level ... 28

5.1 Answering the reading paper at scholarship level ... 28

5.2 Another way of revising for your scholarship exam ... 38

Chapter 6: Writing ... 40

6.1 11+ Composition ... 40

6.2 13+ Writing ... 40

6.3 A note about themes ... 41

6.4 General advice about writing well ... 41

6.5 General advice on writing a story ... 46

6.6 General advice on writing a factual account or description ... 51

6.7 General advice on writing your opinions ... 52

6.8 11+ Writing a book-related composition ... 53

6.9 13+ Response to studied literature ... 56

Chapter 7: Using English accurately 59

7.1 Word classes or 'parts of speech' 59

7.2 Punctuation 63

7.3 Grammar 68

7.4 Spelling 73

Test yourself answers 75

Introduction

This is not a textbook. It is a revision book to help you in the last few months and weeks before you take your entrance exams at 11+ or 13+. Its purpose is to remind you of all you have learned in English lessons and to show you how to write good answers.

Probably, by now, you have already done quite a lot of work from textbooks. This will have widened your knowledge and understanding of English – such a lovely subject with all those delicious words and opportunities to read widely.

Revision – which comes from Latin and means 'looking again' – is just that. You need to spend time looking back at all you have learned so that you can show the examiner what a lot you now understand, know and can do.

There are no facts to memorise in English. It is different from subjects like history, geography or science. The exam tests your ability to read perceptively and to write well and accurately. It examines the skills which you have developed through class work.

This book builds on everything you have learned until now and shows you how to do your best in the exam. It also provides quick reminders of the grammar, punctuation and spelling you have already been taught, as well as the technical terms you need when you are writing about English literature. As you work through these sections – if this is your own copy of the book – it might help and encourage you to tick off the sections as you complete them.

As you go on studying English, your knowledge and understanding builds up and deepens. Think of it as a building on deep foundations to which you keep adding more storeys. That is why much of the material in this book is common to both 11+ and 13+ candidates – although the detail of what's on the exam paper set for the two age groups is different.

Much of the general advice, therefore, is for both groups, followed by examples of how to write high-scoring answers at the two levels.

The syllabus and your exams

Your teacher will have told you what your exams involve. But, to ensure that you are quite clear about it, look carefully at this summary of what your English exams will consist of so that you know exactly what you have to do.

11+

11+ Paper 1: Comprehension exercise on fiction or non-fiction passage. 40 minutes + 5 minutes' reading time. 25 marks

11+ Paper 2: Composition on one of a choice of subjects including the opportunity to write about a book you have read. 40 minutes + 5 minutes' reading time. 25 marks

13+

13+ Paper 1: Comprehension exercise on one or two non-fiction passages AND a second comprehension on a poem or part of a long poem. 1 hour 10 minutes. 50 marks

13+ Paper 2: An essay about a book or other text (such as a play or selection of poems) you have studied AND a composition on a subject you choose from six options on the paper. 1 hour 20 minutes. 50 marks

Scholarship

Scholarship: The ISEB Common Academic Scholarship Examination (CASE) includes comprehension questions on two passages which have some subject matter or ideas in common. 1 hour 45 minutes. 50 marks. The format of papers not set by ISEB may vary.

Further details can be downloaded from the ISEB website: www.iseb.co.uk

A note on Levels 1 and 2

From 2010 the 13+ Paper 1 (Reading) will be split into two levels. A new 'foundation' level will be introduced (Level 1), with Level 2 corresponding to the existing 'standard' Common Entrance specification. Both papers will use the same literary passage but the questions will be different. Although the analytical skills of Level 1 candidates will be tested less rigorously the advice given in this book remains relevant to both levels. All candidates should revise all topics to give themselves the best possible chance in the exam.

How to revise

- Find a quiet place in which to revise. Few of us can do our best work and thinking when there is a lot of distracting background noise. At home, use your bedroom or some other peaceful spot. At school, the library may be best.
- Organise your revision so that you do a section a day for each subject. If you revise some English for a short time each day you will probably have worked pretty thoroughly through what you need to know.
- Don't try to revise the whole of one subject before you move on to another. That way some subjects are bound to get left too late and have to be hurried. You might also have forgotten, by exam time, some of the work you did at the beginning. Aim to keep all your subjects evenly 'on the boil'.
- Don't force yourself to work for hours without a break. Stop for five minutes at least once every half-hour. Research about how people learn has shown that most people absorb more if they do this. Spend your break usefully – some physical exercise is particularly good for refreshing the brain with oxygen.
- Promise yourself a little treat when the exams are over and you can stop revising – perhaps an exciting book which you have been looking forward to reading or a DVD you want to watch. This helps to put you in a better frame of mind for revision.
- Make the most of all the expertise and talent available to you in school. If you really don't understand something, it's sometimes worth asking a teacher other than your own. Every teacher has his or her own way of explaining things and we all learn in different ways. You may find that suddenly you understand something which has always given you trouble.

- Use past papers to familiarise yourself with the format of the exam. You will feel much more confident going into the exam if you know what to expect.
- Do some physical activity every day during your revision. You will not be able to revise effectively if you are not feeling fit and well.
- Eat healthy food while you are revising and don't skip meals. Your brain works better when you give it good fuel.
- Make sure you read as many books as you can while you are revising to improve your own personal word bank.
- Re-read the two or three books you have studied recently and which you are likely to write about in the exam. Remind yourself of any written work you have done on them or notes you have made.
- Make lists of examples of words which have more than one meaning and useful verbs for writing about literature.
- As you revise, practise writing paragraphs consisting of sentences of different lengths and different shapes. Notice and think about sentence length and shape while you're reading too.
- Devise your own sample papers. Then write the sort of questions based on them which you think an examiner would ask. Practise writing answers to your own questions – or swap with someone else.

How to cope with the exam

- Try to get a good night's sleep the night before the exam. You will be able to approach the exam much more positively if you feel refreshed. Don't eat too late the night before and have a good breakfast in the morning.
- Check that you have everything you need to take into the exam. Take at least two pens in case one runs out. Your teacher will tell you if there are any other items you need to take as well.
- If your school allows it, take some water into the exam with you.
- Make sure you read and understand the rubric (instructions and rules) on the front of the exam paper.
- Allow some time at the start to read and consider the questions carefully before writing anything. Don't rush into answering before you have had a chance to think about it.
- Work out how much time you need to allocate to each question. During the exam try not to over-run on one question, leaving too little time for another.
- Read the exam passage(s) right through carefully.
- Look closely at the sentence at the top of the passage which introduces it. It's there to help you.

- If the meanings of any of the words in the passage(s) are given at the bottom to help you, make sure you refer to these as you read.
- Read all the questions you are asked to answer, at least twice.
- Never begin to write your answers before you have read the passage(s) and the questions thoroughly.

For more tips on how to get the best from your revision and exams, see *Study Skills* by Elizabeth Holtom, published by Galore Park.

Useful resources

Study Skills by Elizabeth Holtom, ISBN: 9781902984599
Junior English Book 1 by Andrew Hammond, ISBN: 9781902984827
Junior English Book 1 Answer Book by Andrew Hammond, ISBN: 9781902984872
Junior English Book 2 by Andrew Hammond, ISBN: 9781902984810
Junior English Book 2 Answer Book by Andrew Hammond, ISBN: 9781902984865
Junior English Book 3 by Andrew Hammond, ISBN: 9781902984803
Junior English Book 3 Answer Book by Andrew Hammond, ISBN: 9781902984858
So you really want to learn English Book 1 by Susan Elkin, ISBN: 9781902984537
So you really want to learn English Book 1 Answer Book by Susan Elkin, ISBN: 9781902984568
So you really want to learn English Book 2 by Susan Elkin, ISBN: 9781902984667
So you really want to learn English Book 2 Answer Book by Susan Elkin, ISBN: 9781902984575
So you really want to learn English Book 3 by Susan Elkin, ISBN: 9781902984926
So you really want to learn English Book 3 Answer Book by Susan Elkin, ISBN: 9781902984933

All available from Galore Park: www.galorepark.co.uk.

Chapter 1: Comprehension and reading

1.1 How to approach a fiction or non-fiction comprehension passage

Remember that in English comprehension work there are often no right or wrong answers. There may be several ways of answering a question in your own words. It is your opportunity to show what and how you think. You might even spot something examiners haven't thought of. Even if it is not exactly what the examiner has written on his or her mark sheet, you will get good marks for writing something sensible and thoughtful – as long as it answers the question and you can back up what you say with evidence from the text.

Read the passage

- It may sound obvious, but the first and most important thing you have to do is to read the passage(s) right through carefully.
- Some people find it helps to subvocalise. That means you slow up and read it aloud to yourself in your head – rather than reading it very fast as if it were a story you are reading casually for fun at home. Others prefer to skim-read it once and then read it a second time, more slowly. Most people find it useful to read the passage(s) more than once. Decide which method works best for you.
- Look closely at the sentence at the top of the page which introduces the paragraph. It's there to help you.
- If the meanings of any of the words in the passage(s) are given at the bottom to help you, make sure you refer to these as you read.

Read the questions

- Read all the questions you are asked to answer, at least twice.
- Think about what they mean and make notes if you wish.
- Never begin to write your answers before you have read both the passage(s) and the questions thoroughly.
- You might like to highlight key words in the questions as you read.
- The whole reading process can take several minutes. Do not panic if the person next to you begins writing immediately. Your answers will probably be better than his or hers because you have read and thought carefully before writing them.

Use the right style in your answers

- Answer most questions in full sentences.
- Do not begin with 'because' or with words like 'plus'.

- Use a capital letter at the beginning and a full stop at the end of each whole sentence.
- If your answer needs other punctuation such as commas, then be careful where and how you place them.
- If you are asked for short details or points from a passage (for example to give another word for one that is in the passage to show that you understand it), then you need not use a whole sentence.
- Imitate the style of the passage in your answers but use your own words as much as you can.
- Take great care with spelling. It is particularly careless to misspell a word which is in the passage or questions.
- Be as precise as you can.
- Avoid slang and sloppy expressions such as 'like' (unless you mean similar to), 'cool' (unless you mean at a low-ish temperature) and *never* write 'and stuff'.

1.2 Different types of writing

11+ If you are taking the 11+ papers there is usually just one comprehension passage. It can be fiction or non-fiction. You will probably be told at the top what it is. Among other things it could be:

- part of a novel or short story (look for characters, dialogue, imaginative description and sometimes a story teller who is part of the story)
- part of a real-life story – a biography or autobiography (watch for the writer looking back at, or describing, personal events which happened in the past)
- a news story from a newspaper (quite short with all key information revealed in the opening paragraph rather than held back for suspense)
- an opinion piece from a newspaper, magazine or website (look for 'I think' or 'I believe').

13+ If you are a 13+ candidate your first comprehension passage will not be fiction. It will be taken, for example, from:

- a factual or reference book
- a travel book
- a newspaper, magazine or website
- an instruction manual
- any other non-fiction source.

The second comprehension will be based on a poem, or part of one. It could be:

- by a living poet
- by a recently or long-dead 20th century poet
- a Victorian poem
- a romantic poem (by Keats or Shelley, for example)
- by Shakespeare
- a narrative (story-telling) poem
- a sonnet
- an ode
- or almost any other sort of poem from any period.

You will be told the name of the poet.

If you are a scholarship candidate you will have to answer questions in detail and depth on two different passages – of any type – which can in some way be connected. For example, you might get an extract from one of Charles Dickens's novels (such as *Bleak House*) about the law and a newspaper report from, say, *The Times*, about a recent legal case. Or you might get part of Wordsworth's book-length autobiographical poem 'The Prelude' along with part of the autobiography of Hunter Davies, who – as Wordsworth did – lives in the Lake District.

Answer as fully as you can

Put as much detail into your answers as you can. A good answer may need several sentences, such as in the following sample answers.

Q. *Sample question*

Look at the following sentence about South American screamer birds in the passage:

> *All we knew was that screamers were supposed to be entirely vegetarian, but whenever a butterfly hovered within six feet of Egbert, his whole being seemed to be filled with blood-lust, his eyes would take on a fanatical and most un-vegetarian-like gleam and he would endeavour to stalk it.*
>
> (From *The Drunken Forest* by Gerald Durrell, 1956)

Q. Explain the meaning of 'his eyes would take on a fanatical and most un-vegetarian-like gleam.'

A. *Sample answer*

A. Although screamer birds are plant eaters, this particular one ('Egbert') seems strangely interested in watching and trying to catch butterflies. The writer is intrigued because such determination and the intent look in the bird's eyes humorously suggest that it is hard to believe it does not regard the butterfly as prey.

- Write a full answer using your own words, if you can.
- If the answer is too short and simple it will not get many marks.

Your turn

Now try the sample question on page 3 for yourself and compare your answer with the sample answer above. Don't forget the tips above.

Highlight key words

- If you are asked to summarise information from the passage, highlight the key words in the passage.
- Then sum up whatever points you are asked about in your own words, quoting short phrases to make sure that your answer stays close to the passage.
- Do not put these phrases on separate lines. Weave them into your sentences and put inverted commas around them.
- Remember you are like a scientist. Look in the passage for evidence to 'prove' what you write.
- Don't forget that the purpose of all this is for you to show that you have understood the passage.

Q. *Sample question*

Darkness swallowed me; the branches arched high overhead; I saw only glimpses of the paler sky through their tracery. My feet crunched beech mast. I smelled the coolness of the mossy earth and heard the trickle of water close by. As my eyes accustomed themselves to dimmer light, I saw that here, on the lower ground, a faint mist hung in the air, trapped perhaps beneath the trees. I must be careful not to stray from the path, which I could only dimly discern; but before many minutes had passed, wrought iron gates reared ahead of me, set in a wall of flint. Though I had reached the edge of the wood my way was barred. The gate, must, however, be unlocked, as my arrival was expected.

(From *Set in Stone* by Linda Newbery, 2006)

Q. Sum up the writer's thoughts and impressions as he approaches the gates.

A. *Sample answer*

A. All the narrator's senses are aroused by the dark, mysterious wood he is passing through at dusk on his way to gates leading to a property where he is an expected visitor. He hears 'crunched beech mast' under his feet and the sound of water nearby. He smells 'mossy earth' and can see trees, mist and, eventually, the big, rather sinister ('reared') gates in front of him. He seems to be nervous because he is in a place which is new to him. That is why he is alert to every sensation around him.

Your turn

Now try the sample question on page 4 for yourself and compare your answer with the sample answer above.

Look at the context

You will usually be asked at least one question about the meaning of a word, or words, as used in the passage.

Many words in English have several meanings according to how they are used. Look at the word 'mast' in the passage above from *Set in Stone*. There it means the nuts produced by beech trees and sometimes fed to pigs. But the word 'mast' also means the upright which supports the sails on a ship.

And think about the following:

- game, **set** and match; **set** the table for tea
- an **invalid** lying in bed; an **invalid** bus ticket
- having to **boot** up your computer; emptying the car **boot**
- the **minute** hand on your watch; a **minute** doll's house.

List, as part of your revision, other examples of words which have more than one meaning.

So, if you are asked the meaning of a word (or phrase) in a passage, it is very important to look at the way it is used – its context.

For example:

To this address, my aunt had listened with the closest of attention.

(From *David Copperfield* by Charles Dickens, 1850).

Q. What does the word 'address' mean?

You might write:

A. The 'address' is words which have just been said – or addressed – to the speaker's aunt.

Do not consider the more usual 21st century meaning of 'address' as someone's home or personal email contact. It is also another word for a formal speech such as a sermon in church. Ignore this too in your answer.

Here is another example:

Some of the crocuses were shooting, and striped dark green leaves showed through the grass which was winter thin and short.

(From *A Kid for Two Farthings* by Wolf Mankowitz, 1953)

Q. What does the word 'shooting' mean?

A good answer would be:

A. The word 'shooting' tells us that the crocuses were thrusting their leaves out of the soil in such a sudden and aggressive way that it reminds the writer of bullets from guns.

Sometimes you will simply be asked to give another word or phrase which means the same as a word in the passage. Again, think about the context and ignore any other meaning(s) the word may have.

For example:

In every aircraft there is an electronic **monitor** which oversees the automatic pilot and gives an early warning of possible problems.

Q. What does the word 'monitor' mean?

Your answer could, among other possibilities, be one of these:

A. mechanism
device
checker
supervisor

If you happen to know that a monitor is also a sort of lizard, a prefect in school or that it can be used as a verb – don't worry about it. Concentrate on the way the word is used in the passage.

When explaining the meaning of words, the secret is to remove the word in the passage. Then try your word in the gap – like a jigsaw piece. If it fits – and the sentence still means the same thing – then it is a good answer.

Here is another example:

Perfume is a **major** item of French industry and commerce.

Q. What does the word 'major' mean?

Some of the answers you could give are:

A. important
significant
big
valuable

Don't worry, obviously, about 'major' also being an army rank.

Use evidence from the passage

You must be able to prove, or back up, every answer with evidence from the passage. So:

- Refer in your own words to what the writer says.
- Quote single words and short phrases (with inverted commas around them) woven into your answers.
- Look for, and comment on, parts of the passage in which the writer hints at something, but perhaps doesn't, for some reason, say it straightforwardly. In other words, ask yourself what lies under or behind the writer's words. You may have been taught to call this the 'subtext'.
- In fiction, look at what characters say and at what the narrator says.

Q. *Sample question*

Jody leaped forward and plunged down the hill. The wet ground muffled his steps and the brush hid him. When he arrived it was all over. The first buzzard sat on the pony's head. Jody plunged into the circle like a cat. The Black brotherhood rose in a cloud, but the big one on the pony's head was too late. As it hopped along to take off, Jody caught its wing tip and pulled it down. It was nearly as big as he was. The free wing crashed into his face with the force of a club but he hung on. The claws fastened on his leg and the wing elbows battered his head on either side. Jody groped wildly with his free hand; his fingers found the neck of the struggling bird. The red eyes looked into his face, calm and fearless and fierce: he held the bird's neck to the ground with one hand while with the other he found a piece of sharp white quartz. He struck again and again until the buzzard lay dead. He was still beating the dead bird when Billy Buck pulled him off and held him to calm his shaking.

(Slightly abridged from *The Red Pony* by John Steinbeck, 1937)

Q. Why does Jody kill the buzzard?

A. *Sample answer*

A. Jody is beside himself with rage and distress because his pony has died and, although he 'leaped' and 'plunged', in his hurry he is too late to see the animal's last moments. So he is cross with himself. Buzzards feed on freshly dead flesh and a group – looking sinister and greedy ('black brotherhood') – has been waiting near the dying, now dead, pony. Although he is quite young – the bird is not much smaller than he is – Jody launches a frenzied attack on the bird which has already perched on the pony's head ready to feed. He is not thinking rationally. The writer tells us that Jody 'groped wildly' and then he goes on hitting the bird with a piece of rock even after it is dead. He is probably full of adrenaline and extra strength because he is so upset and angry about his pony's death. He manages to hold onto the big bird despite its struggling and kills it even though it claws his leg and tries to beat him off with its strong wings. This is the action of a boy who is frustrated and angry and wanting – or needing – to take his feelings out on something. If he lives in the country he must know that the buzzards don't kill ponies.

A full answer will make good use of evidence from the passage.

Your turn

Now try the sample question on page 7 for yourself and compare your answer with the sample answer above. Don't forget the tip above.

Manage your time and check your work

- Making the best use of your time is one of the most important things to get right in an exam. It can make a big difference to your marks. If you don't spread your time properly across all the questions, don't finish or don't check your work before you hand in your paper you have not shown the examiner what you can really do.
- You MUST leave a few minutes at the end to check your work. Correct any obvious spelling mistakes. Make sure every sentence ends with a full stop. Put in any words you may have left out. Sort out any other slips you can spot. Make quick improvements where you can.
- So, keep an eye on the clock in the room. Split the time into little blocks for each question (some answers will be shorter than others). Make sure you have 5 minutes or so left at the end to read over your work.
- In a 40 minutes + 5 minutes' reading time 11+ paper, spend no more than 35 minutes writing. Use the last 5 minutes to read through everything you have written.
- In a 1 hour 10 minutes 13+ paper, allow 7 or 8 minutes to read and make notes at the beginning. Write for no more than 56 minutes (28 minutes for each of the two sections). Use the last 6 or 7 minutes to check your work.
- In a 1 hour 45 minutes scholarship paper, leave at least 10 minutes' checking time at the end.

Summary

You should now know the following:

1. The different types of comprehension exercises you are likely to come across in your exam.
2. How to approach the comprehension passage in your exam.
3. The style of answer you should use to respond to the questions.
4. How to work out the context of words which have different meanings.

Test yourself

Before moving on to the next chapter, make sure you can answer the following questions. Suggested answers are at the back of the book.

1. Write down two different meanings for each of the following words:
   (a) blow
   (b) dart
   (c) spirit
   (d) deck

2. Write down a different word which has the same meaning for each of the following:
   (a) rage
   (b) strike
   (c) gloomy
   (d) weary

Chapter 2: Reading at 11+

11+

In this chapter we look at how to cope with the comprehension paper at 11+.

2.1 11+ Comprehension exercise on a fiction passage

The main purpose of this part of the exam is to give you the chance to show that you can:

- read a substantial passage without help
- write answers to questions independently
- show your understanding of the passage in various ways.

In your exam you will have 5 minutes' reading and planning time followed by 40 minutes to produce your answers, which should be written in full sentences.

The total number of marks available is 25. Remember to give more time, and to write in more detail, in your answers to the questions which carry the most marks – in this example, questions 8 and 9.

Q. *Sample question*

In this extract from *The Swan Kingdom* by Zoë Marriott, Alexandra's quest leads her to a remote cottage.

1 *Turning to look up the hill, I saw a curl of smoke rising behind the wildly overgrown hedge near by, and the peak of a thatched roof. Reaching out, I could feel the presence of animals, bored and not very well fed, and – at last! – people, two of them. I offered a brief prayer to the Ancestors that the farmers would be friendly, and walked on, Mare following faithfully behind me.*

5 *I rounded the hedge and stopped dead in shock. I stared, Mare nosing at my shoulder curiously.*

I saw not the square, stone Midland dwelling that I had been expecting, but a Kingdom-style wood-frame house, curved in the shape of the long oak boughs used to build it, walls of wattle and limewash, and thatching that ended only a few feet from the ground. To one side a pair of bored cows shared a small byre, and chickens clucked on the gravelled area before it. It looked
10 *incredibly homely and inviting to my eyes; but who would have built such a house here?*

Before I could even begin to answer my own question, a young boy rounded the corner of the byre, a wooden bucket in his arms. He was large for his age, which I had thought was about eight or nine, but skinny. He had a round face and straw-coloured hair that poked up in all directions as if he had run his fingers through it.

15 *He froze when he saw me, his arms going limp and allowing grain to spill out from the bucket onto the gravel. The chickens converged on him in a squawking crowd, but his muddy-brown eyes never left my face. I was a little surprised by his look of stunned bewilderment, but supposed he might be frightened at the unexpected arrival of a stranger. I tried a tentative smile to see if it would reassure him. If anything his eyes grew rounder.*

20 *'Hello,' I said.*

He gulped and carried on staring.

'It's all right. I got lost in the woods, and wondered if you could tell me where I am,' I said quietly, using the calm tone I adopted with frightened animals.

He blinked and stared some more. Did I look that awful? I raised a hand self-consciously to my
25 *hair, which was escaping its braid as fast as it could and clustering around my face in twiddly red curls, and tucked as much of it behind my ears as would fit.*

'Is something wrong?' I asked finally. 'Should I go away again?'

The boy shook his head frantically, almost dropping the bucket entirely as he started into action. 'No, no, Lady! Just ... you just wait here, Lady. I'll get my ma!'

30 *He ran to the house, scattering grain left and right, and disappeared through the open doorway. I heard the sound of a woman's voice raised – likely telling the boy off for getting mud and grain all over her floor – and then there was quiet.*

A moment later, a short, middle-aged woman with untidy straw-coloured hair appeared in the doorway, wiping her hands on her apron. The boy was behind her, whispering frantically and
35 *pointing as he came into view. The expression on her face – one of mixed curiosity and impatience – transformed when she saw me into shock and ... oh, dear, was that awe?*

'Lady ...' she whispered, almost to herself, her eyes as wide as her son's had been. 'Oh, Lady. How did you come to be here?'

Q.

1. What is Mare? How do you know? (1 mark)
2. Explain in your own words what the boy is doing when Alexandra meets him. (1 mark)
3. What surprises Alexandra about the boy's mother? (2 marks)
4. Use your own words to describe Alexandra's first impression of the cottage. (3 marks)
5. What do you think Alexandra would like these people to do for her? (3 marks)
6. What does the writer mean by 'the chickens converged on him in a squawking crowd' in line 16? (2 marks)
7. How can you tell that this novel is set in a fantasy world without any of the main religions we recognise today? (1 mark)
8. What do we learn about Alexandra, her appearance and reputation from the reaction of the boy and his mother? You may wish to mention how the writer uses Alexandra as the narrator, the use of dialogue and descriptions. (6 marks)
9. By the end of the passage what impressions have you formed of Alexandra? Give reasons and examples to support your answers. (6 marks)

A. *Sample answers*

1. Mare is an animal, almost certainly a female horse, which is why Alexandra calls her 'Mare'. This can be deduced from the passage because she is 'following faithfully' and she noses Alexandra's shoulder – both examples of horse-like behaviour.

2. The boy is about to feed the chickens with grain from a bucket.

3. The boy's mother is almost as shocked to see Alexandra as the boy had been. At first she seems ordinary but then her face changes and her eyes go wide. She seems very startled and looks at Alexandra as if she is being visited by someone very special. This is not what Alexandra was expecting from an adult.

4. Half hidden by a large straggly hedge, the thatched cottage has curved walls because its main support is long oak boughs. The walls are based on a woven framework ('wattle') covered in clay and lime. The overhanging edge of the roof almost touches the ground and there is a separate building for cattle ('byre') next to it.

5. Alexandra is looking for a friendly welcome ('a brief prayer to the Ancestors that the farmers would be friendly.') in the 'incredibly inviting' cottage. She wants to be greeted like an ordinary human being. She is not pleased to see awe in the woman's face. She is afraid she looks scruffy, which is why she tries to tidy her hair, so she would probably be grateful for washing facilities and perhaps some clean clothes. There is a lot about animals and food in this passage so she may also be hungry and hoping that they will offer her a meal. Her horse, Mare, needs somewhere to rest too.

6. The boy is so shocked so see Alexandra that he accidentally lets the bucket tip so some of the chickens' grain falls out. The birds see it and gather excitedly and noisily round to peck up what they can.

7. Instead of praying to God for help she prays to the Ancestors. She must have been brought up in a different religious system.

8. Alexandra seems to look very strange and have some kind of magical aura about her. The writer tells us that the boy freezes and that a look of 'stunned bewilderment' crosses his face as soon as he sees her. His shock is made even clearer because for a minute he does not (cannot?) speak. Alexandra tries to address him normally but, we are told, he can only gulp. Then when his mother appears she looks impatient and curious – until she sees Alexandra. The woman is shocked and, Alexandra thinks, awed. She has presumably recognised Alexandra as someone important and cannot understand why she has arrived at the cottage. She and the boy both call her 'Lady' very respectfully.

9. Alexandra – with her plaited red hair ('escaping its braid') – must be determined and strong. She has obviously been on some kind of long, lonely and difficult journey and, having come through the woods and down the hill, is much relieved to find this cottage. She is skilled with animals. She manages Mare and has a technique ('calm tone') for frightened animals which she also tries out on the terrified boy. She has pleasant

manners and speaks politely to the boy. She isn't conceited and does not want to be treated as someone special. She is uncomfortable when the woman mutters 'Oh Lady. How did you come to be here' under her breath – almost as if it were a prayer.

- Make sure you include enough detail to answer the question fully.
- Refer closely to the text and use it as evidence to back up your answer, but make sure you use your own words.
- Try and weave relevant quotations into your answer.
- Make sure you use formal expressions and avoid slang/sloppy words.
- Leave enough time to check your work for grammar and spelling errors, and that no words are missing from your answer – make sure you revise punctuation and spelling rules.

Your turn

Now try the sample questions on page 11 for yourself and compare your answers with the sample answers above. Don't forget the tips above.

2.2 11+ Comprehension exercise on a non-fiction passage

Let's look at a typical 11+ exercise on a non-fiction passage.

Q. *Sample question*

This article, which appeared in the *Daily Mail* on 12th June 2007, is about a prep school with an unusual headship arrangement:

1 ***Headmaster and Missus***

Heads don't need to have been teachers according to a government-commissioned report which infuriated the teaching unions recently.

Schools, it said, simply need good managers of organisations.

5 *Whatever anyone thinks about that brave suggestion, change is certainly in the wind. Too few people are applying for headships, especially at primary level.*

And many schools are not competently led – witness all the schools which are failing or in 'special measures.'

If the government wants to consider new ways of managing schools, what about appointing
10 *husband and wife teams to do the job jointly?*

David and Sarah Telfer have been joint heads of Witham Hall, an independent preparatory school in Lincolnshire, for nine years.

They are not job sharers. They are both designated 'head teacher,' each with an appropriate full-time salary.

15 *'Our skills are complementary,' they say. Mr Telfer, a passionate Scot, who manages the senior part of the school is a former maths teacher inclined to science and problem solving.*

Mrs Telfer's strengths are English and the arts. She manages the younger part of the school, although both are designated heads across the whole school. The Telfers have taught in a range of schools in the North East, Kent and Sussex, including several state schools.

20 *They live in an on-site house at Witham Hall which has 230 pupils, including 35 boarders and over 90 occasional boarders.*

Witham Hall is an astonishingly successful school which may be partly due to the innovative way it is managed. It is not selective.

There are no entrance tests. Sixty pupils have special needs and are helped by 'learning support.'
25 *One pupil has a full statement of special needs which means he has a full-time helper assigned to him.*

And yet every pupil for many years has passed the Common Entrance Exam – the tests taken by children in independent schools at 11 or 13 to transfer to senior school.

'They all get into the schools of their choice too,' says Mr Telfer who sends pupils to schools like
30 *Oundle, Uppingham and Oakham. Occasionally a child goes further afield to Marlborough, Shrewsbury, Ampleforth or Eton.*

Many get scholarships to senior schools – 20 this year which is more than two thirds of the year group.

'We take nearly every art scholarship for miles around,' says Mr Telfer showing me astonishing,
35 *full size sculptures of dragons, horses, cricketers and otters made by 12 year olds under the tutelage of an outstandingly charismatic art teacher.*

The school also gets an above-average number of music and academic scholarships.

No wonder the recent report by the Independent Schools Inspectorate, which works in liaison with Ofsted, uses the word 'excellent' in nearly every paragraph.

40 *So what is it about joint headship which achieves all this?*

'We see the school as a family, so it's appropriate to have a mother and father figure at the top,' says Mrs Telfer. The Telfers have an adult daughter and son of their own.

There is a sensitive, caring and friendly – but businesslike – rapport between the Telfers and the staff and pupils. Both make time for a word with almost every child and adult they pass and, of
45 *course, they know everyone by name.*

Because there are two of them, capacity is doubled. So they have an unusually high knowledge of what is going on in the school.

Mrs Telfer, for example, knows exactly what is being taught to which class in the nursery and pre-prep department (age three to eight) and can discuss the work with any child or teacher.

50 *Because they have been together a long time (they met at teacher training college and have been married for 34 years) the Telfers have an instinctive understanding of, and respect for, each other's strengths and concerns. And they don't suffer from the isolation which besets many head teachers and other top managers.*

The Telfers happen both to be teachers, but it wouldn't have to be so. The responsibilities could
55 *be shared in various ways – why not a business manager and a teacher, or a police officer and a teacher or an army officer and a teacher?*

Q. 1. What does Mr Telfer mean by 'our skills are complementary'? (1 mark)

2. Explain the meaning of 'joint headship'. (1 mark)

3. What was the reaction of teaching unions to the suggestion that a school head does not need to be a teacher first? Why do you think the unions felt like this? (4 marks)

4. What does the passage tell you about Mr and Mrs Telfer's life outside school? (3 marks)

5. Why do you think the government ordered a report about headship? (3 marks)

6. What, according to this passage, are the advantages of a school being run by a husband and wife team? (6 marks)

7. Summarise the evidence that Witham Hall is an unusually good school. (7 marks)

A. *Sample answers*

1. Mr Telfer means that he and his wife are good at different things. If there is something one of them finds difficult then the other can probably do it. So their strengths fit together.

2. Mr and Mrs Telfer are both head teachers. They are a team of two which runs the school. They are equal and they each get a full-time head's salary.

3. The teaching unions – clubs or organisations which advise teachers and represent their interests – did not like the suggestion that anyone but a teacher could become a head. They reacted crossly. This was probably because they thought that it could mean outsiders coming in and taking top jobs which ought to go to teachers. They may also have been worried that people who had not been teachers would not understand how to educate children properly.

4. Mr and Mrs Telfer met when they were young while they were training to be teachers. They have been married since 1973. They have two grown up children – a daughter and a son. They live in a house which is part of Witham Hall School.

5. The government was probably worried because it has vacancies for headships which teachers aren't applying for. So it has to think of other ways of running its schools.

6. If you have two heads instead of one you get twice as much work done. That means that the couple can both move around different parts of the school every day and, between them, know every pupil and teacher and what is going on in lessons. They can talk to teachers and children about their work and help them with it. Because Mr and Mrs Telfer live together all the time they can talk to each other about school matters and sort out problems whenever it's convenient. They can probably get problems solved more quickly and easily than in a school where most teachers, including the head (one person), go their separate ways in the evenings or during the holidays. Heads who do the job by themselves sometimes say they feel lonely because they have nobody equal to talk to. A husband and wife team makes being a head a less solitary position. It boils down to 'Two heads are better than one' as in the saying.

7. All Witham Hall pupils pass the Common Entrance exam. The school does not, however, set entrance tests. It takes children even if they have some learning difficulties – as nearly a quarter of the pupils do. So we can be sure that the teachers teach the pupils well if, by the time the children leave, they have made enough progress to pass difficult exams. The school's pupils also win a large number of scholarships to senior schools, particularly in art. The journalist who wrote the article and visited the school was impressed by the art. She describes 'astonishing, full size sculptures of dragons, horses, cricketers and otters made by 12 year olds.' Witham Hall pupils are not disappointed when they apply to senior schools. They are offered places at schools which they or their parents choose, such as Oundle and Uppingham. When school inspectors visited Witham Hall they described almost everything it does as 'excellent.' The article suggests that such success may be because the school has a husband and wife team as joint heads.

- Make sure you do not misspell anything given in the question.
- Include enough depth and detail to obtain all the marks.
- Make sure you quote accurately where it is appropriate.

Your turn

Now try the sample questions on page 15 for yourself and compare your answers with the sample answers above. Don't forget the tips above.

Summary

You should now know the following:

1. How to approach the comprehension questions on a fiction passage of the 11+ exam.
2. How to approach the comprehension questions on a non-fiction passage of the 11+ exam.

Chapter 3: Reading at 13+ (non-fiction)

13+

We now move on to reading at 13+. At this level, you need to be able to cope with non-fiction passages and poetry. We begin with non-fiction.

3.1 13+ Exercise on a non-fiction text

You have 1 hour and 10 minutes for the non-fiction paper.

There are 50 marks available:

- 25 for reading and answering questions on one or two passages which are not fiction
- 25 for reading and answering questions on a poem or part of a poem.

The non-fiction section gives you the chance to show that you:

- understand the passage(s)
- can use what you have read to illustrate your answers
- can work things out from your reading
- can see how the writer(s) is/are working
- can say what you think, based on what you have read
- know how language style – such as grammar, word order and punctuation – can change meaning
- can make comparisons.

Q. *Sample question*

Here are two short passages about the work of Guglielmo Marconi. The first is Marconi's own account. The second is an explanation from a modern science book.

Passage A

1 *Shortly before mid-day I placed the single earphone to my ear and started listening. The receiver on the table before me was very crude – a few coils and condensers and a coherer – no valves, no amplifiers, not even a crystal. But I was at last on the point of putting the correctness of all my beliefs to the test. The answer came at 12.30 when I heard, faintly but distinctly, pip-pip-pip. I*
5 *handed the phone to Kemp: 'Can you hear anything?' I asked. 'Yes,' he said, 'the letter S' – he could hear it. I knew then that all my anticipations had been justified. The electric waves sent out into space from Poldhu had traversed the Atlantic – the distance, enormous as it seemed then, of 1,700 miles – unimpeded by the curvature of the earth. The result meant much more to me than the mere successful realisation of an experiment. As Sir Oliver Lodge has stated it was an*
10 *epoch in history. I now felt for the first time absolutely certain that the day would come when*

mankind would be able to send messages without wires not only across the Atlantic but between the farthermost ends of the earth.

(By Guglielmo Marconi)

Passage B

1 *It is 12th December 1901. In St John's, Newfoundland, on the east coast of Canada, a team of people is struggling to raise a long aerial into the stormy skies. Supported by balloons and kites, the aerial is at last raised. Miraculously, it picks up faint signals – the letter S in Morse code. The signal comes from Poldhu in Cornwall, England. It is the first international radio broadcast.*

5 *The driving force behind the first transatlantic radio transmission was the Italian inventor Guglielmo Marconi. He had been experimenting with sending radio, or 'wireless' messages, for six years. In December 1901 he proved that radio could be a new way for the whole world to communicate.*

Today radio stations in every country broadcast programmes to billions of people. And two-way
10 *radio links connect mobile phones, aircraft with airports, ships with the shore and spacecraft with Earth.*

In a radio studio microphones make an electrical 'copy' of the sound being recorded. This is called a sound signal. The sound signal is combined with a more powerful signal called the carrier wave. The combined signal goes to a transmitter, a metal antenna on a tall mast that sends out the
15 *signal as radio waves. The radio waves travel through the air to your radio receiver, where an electrical circuit, called a demodulator, extracts the original sound.*

(From *The Young Oxford Encyclopedia of Science*)

Q.

1. What do you understand by (a) coherer and (b) demodulator? It will help you to look at the way these words are used in the passages. (2 marks)
2. What was Marconi's achievement and why was it important? (3 marks)
3. How does the writer of Passage B make Marconi's work seem dramatic in the first paragraph? (4 marks)
4. What do you think Sir Oliver Lodge means by 'an epoch in history?' How far was he right? (4 marks)
5. What do you notice about the style of Marconi's own writing in Passage A? You should write down and discuss quotations in your answer. (6 marks)
6. Compare the two extracts. Which is the most informative? Explain your reasons carefully. (6 marks)

A. *Sample answers*

1. I haven't seen either of these words before but I think a coherer must be something which links or sticks the coils and condensers together (like cohesive and adhesive). A demodulator is probably a device which breaks down (from the prefix de- and words like deconstruct and deform) the moving radio waves in order to get the sound out.

2. Marconi sent the first radio signal from one country to another. It travelled 1700 miles west from Cornwall to Canada. Although it was only one faint morse code signal, the important thing was that Marconi and his colleagues could hear it. It was important because it proved it was possible. And it was the first step in leading the way to modern communications such as radio broadcasts, air traffic control, mobile phones, radio links between space craft and earth, and many other things. Marconi knew at the time that his work would have far-reaching effects. He was 'absolutely certain that the day would come when mankind would be able to send messages without wires not only across the Atlantic but between the farthermost ends of the earth.'

3. The writer uses short sentences. This makes the rhythm jerky and breathy as if something very exciting is unfolding. He also starts with the date because this was a date which people would always remember as it was a turning point. He uses the present tense ('The signal comes', 'It is') which makes the tone very immediate as if it's happening now and the reader is there with the writer and with Marconi. The style is a bit like news reporting in a newspaper. The writer drops back into the past tense in the usual way in the second paragraph which is much less dramatic. It is an effective way of starting a piece of non-fiction writing because it draws the reader in.

4. Sir Oliver Lodge meant that the sending of the first radio signal was an important time in history, now that people could communicate in this new way. He was right about the new era because a century later nearly everyone uses 'wireless' signals all the time – in phones, computers and in many other ways.

5. Marconi is writing a personal, first-hand account of what happened. It is meant to be an accurate record so that people in the future will understand just how it was. That is why he begins with a simple style giving the time and describing exactly what he did. '... I placed the single earphone to my ear and started listening.' He uses straightforward verbs such as 'placed' and 'started'. Only in the second sentence does he use scientific jargon ('coils and condensers and a coherer') because he has to explain precisely, but the grammar is still simple. Marconi was risking making himself look silly with this experiment and you can sense his nervousness in 'putting the correctness of all my beliefs to the test.' The use of direct speech in the conversation with Kemp is effective because it adds to the drama – like a bit of dialogue in a play. His style becomes much more reflective in the final long sentence: 'I now felt for the first time absolutely certain that the day would come when mankind would be able to send messages without wires not only across the Atlantic but between the farthermost ends of the earth.' Words like 'mankind' and 'farthermost' give this sentence a rhetorical feel as if it were part of a memorable speech.

He is remembering something very big and important so he uses a style which moves from factual to imaginative.

6. Passage B was probably written quite recently because it mentions modern developments such as mobile phones and spacecraft. The technology which Marconi started has changed and developed enormously since 1901, so inevitably Passage B is more informative. It also explains very clearly how microphones work and how radio waves are transmitted. On the other hand Passage A is very interesting because it gives a sense of how Marconi actually felt on the day he listened in Canada to a signal sent from Britain. In general Passage B is more scientific and Passage A is more personal, although Passage B tries to be dramatic at first and Passage B explains the science of how the test was set up. Passage B is able to shift from 1901 to 'today' whereas Passage A can only describe what happened then and what might happen in the future.

- For a question such as 1 above, no answer means no mark. If you make a sensible guess from the context (as the question advises) the examiner might give you at least part of the mark.
- When you are asked to compare one thing with another use words and phrases such as:

although	despite
on the other hand	besides
besides which	whereas
however	nevertheless
nonetheless	in spite of

Try not to write first about X then about Y and then one sentence comparing them. It is much better to compare X and Y throughout your answer, point by point.

Your turn

Now try the sample questions on page 18 for yourself and compare your answers with the sample answers above. Don't forget the tips above.

Summary

You should now know the following:

1. How to approach the comprehension questions on a non-fiction passage of the 13+ exam.
2. How to compare two different passages.

Chapter 4: Reading at 13+ (poetry)

13+

Now that you have seen how best to cope with the non-fiction passages, let us look at the poetry section of the 13+ exam.

4.1 Revising the 'tools' of poetry

There are a number of 'tools' which you need to have at your disposal when tackling questions on poetry. Here are some of the most important.

Metaphor

The comparison of one thing with another by pretending that the thing described really is what it is being compared with.

Metaphors are not **literally** true. Like personification or a simile (see below) a metaphor is a form of image. The adjective 'metaphorical' and the adverb 'metaphorically' are useful too.

Examples:

1. *The wind was a torrent of darkness*
2. *... down the ribbon of moonlight*

(both from 'The Highwayman' by Alfred Noyes)

Simile

A comparison of one thing with another which makes it clear that it is a comparison by using the words 'like' or 'as'.

It is another sort of image.

Examples:

1. *sodden **as** the bed of an ancient lake*
2. *... **like** hammered lead*

(both from 'November' by Ted Hughes)

Personification

The giving of human qualities and abilities to non-humans.

Poets often personify things as a way of describing them. It creates an image or picture in the reader's mind.

Examples:

1. *The winds were lovesick with her*

(*Antony and Cleopatra* by William Shakespeare)

2. *… the moon walked the night*

('Silver' by Walter de la Mare)

Alliteration

The repetition of the same letter (or sometimes sound) at the beginning of neighbouring words.

You can also use the adjective 'alliterative'.

Examples:

1. *… downward* ***s****moke, the* ***s****lender* ***s****tream*

('The Lotos Eaters' by Alfred Lord Tennyson)

2. *And through his* ***b****ritches the* ***b****lue winds* ***b****low*

('Timothy Winters' by Charles Causley)

Assonance

The repetition of the same vowel sound (not necessarily spelt the same way) inside neighbouring words.

You can also use the adjective 'assonant'.

Examples:

1. *pl****u****mp,* ***u****npecked cherries*

('Goblin Market' by Christina Rossetti)

2. ***I****'ve l****i****ce in m****y*** *tunic and a cold in m****y*** *nose*

('Roman Wall Blues' by W. H. Auden)

Symbol

An object which stands for something else, like a badge or emblem.

A national flag is a symbol of a country.

Examples:

1. In 'The Rime of the Ancient Mariner' by Samuel Taylor Coleridge the narrator shoots an albatross and has to wear it round his neck as a punishment. The bird is a symbol of sin.
2. In 'The merry bells ring / To welcome the spring' ('The Echoing Green' by William Blake) the bells are a simple symbol of spring.

Irony

Sarcasm or exaggeration or pretending to believe something which is certainly not true to make a point.

It is often 'dry' and funny.

Example:

Within the human world I know
Such goings on could not be so,
For human beings only do
What their religion tells them to.

('Diary of a Church Mouse' by John Betjeman)

The poet really means that most people are hypocrites who do what they like.

Rhythm

The musical pattern of beats, stressed sounds, unstressed sounds and pauses which give a poem its shape.

It can be regular or free.

Examples:

1. *Four o'clock strikes,*
   There's a rising hum,
   Then the doors fly open.
   The children come

('Out of School' by Hal Summers)

The lines above have a regular rhythm with two strong beats in each line.

2. *Glory be to God for dappled things*
   For skies of couple-colour as a brinded cow

('Pied Beauty' by Gerard Manley Hopkins)

The lines above have an irregular rhythm.

Rhyme

Patterns made by words which have the same or similar-sound endings.

There are several sorts of rhyme.

Examples:

1. *The Miller was a chap of sixteen st***one***.*
   *A great stout fellow big in brawn and b***one**

(*The Canterbury Tales* by Geoffrey Chaucer translated by Nevil Coghill)

These lines have a full rhyme.

2. *My last dear fuel of life to heap upon my s**oul***
And kindle my will to a flame that shall consume
*Their dross if indifference and take the t**oll***

('Last Lesson of the Afternoon' by D. H. Lawrence)

These lines have a half, or feminine, rhyme.

3. *Where the wh**eat** is sw**eet** as an angel's **feet***

('Cowboy Song' by Charles Causley)

This line has an internal rhyme. The rhyming words are within rather than at the ends of the line.

4.2 Comprehension exercise on a poem

The poetry question is your chance to show that you:

- are aware of how language is used in poetry
- can write what you think based on your reading of the poem
- understand how poets show the reader what they are feeling
- have learned about metaphor, simile, personification, symbol, irony, alliteration, assonance, rhythm and rhyme.

Q. *Sample question*

Sunken Evening

1 *The green light floods the city square –*
A sea of fowl and feathered fish,
Where squalls of rainbirds dive and splash
And gusty sparrows chop the air.

5 *Submerged, the prawn-blue pigeons feed*
In sandy grottoes round the Mall,
And crusted lobster-buses crawl
Among the fountains' silver weed.

10 *There, like a wreck, with mast and bell,*
The torn church settles by the bow,
While phosphorescent starlings stow
Their mussel shells along the hull.

15 *The oyster-poet, drowned but dry,*
Rolls a black pearl between his bones;
The typist, trapped by telephones,
Gazes in bubbles at the sky.

Till, with the dark, the shallows run,
And homeward surges tide and fret –
The slow night trawls its heavy net
And hauls the clerk to Surbiton.

(By Laurie Lee 1914–1997)

Q. 1. What are the starlings doing and why are they phosphorescent? (3 marks)

2. Explain what the poet is comparing the city with. Refer closely to several words from different verses in your answer. (4 marks)

3. Re-read the third verse. Why does the narrator think the typist is trapped and why is the poet compared with an oyster? Refer closely to the poem to support your ideas. (4 marks)

4. What changes in the last verse and how does the poet describe it? (4 marks)

5. The poet doesn't tell us the exact place that this poem describes. Where do you think it is? Write down at least three quotations to support your answer. (5 marks)

6. Imagine you are a clerk who lives in Surbiton. Write an account of your journey home. (You should write at least one full paragraph.) (5 marks)

A. *Sample answers*

1. The starlings are flying in and out of the hollows and spaces in the walls of the church, carrying bits and pieces. The poet imagines them bringing mussel shells to a wreck as if the birds were underwater creatures. Their feathers have a multi-coloured sheen which reminds the poet of the shiny phosphorescence sometimes seen on the surface of the sea.

2. The poet is comparing the city with the sea. Because the light is green it is like an underwater scene. In this metaphor the birds are 'feathered fishes' (a good expression because of the alliteration which makes them sound very light). The slow (red?) buses are compared with lobsters and the blue-ish grey pigeons with prawns. The fountains in the square with their spraying water look like water weed and the wide road nearby has 'sandy grottoes'. The church is described as a wreck (perhaps it was damaged – maybe in a war?) with a long shape which resembles the hull of a ship.

3. The typist has to stay at her desk because she must answer the telephone. It is as if she were trapped on the sea bed so she gazes longingly toward the surface of the water and the sky because that would be freedom. All she can see is bubbles which symbolise something very fragile which soon disappears. The poet is like an oyster because he has a hard grey crusty shell but with something precious – the poem – inside like an oyster's pearl.

4. The last verse hangs on its first word – the adverb 'till' – which is a turning point to show that the poem is about to move off in a different direction. It is now dark and time for workers to go home. The poet imagines the tide going out as the city empties so that the workers are washed out of the deep sea and stranded. Night, which 'trawls its heavy net', is personified as a fisherman dragging the workers like fish through shallow waters towards their homes on the outskirts of the city.

5. I think the poet is imagining the Trafalgar Square area of London. He mentions 'the Mall' which feeds into Trafalgar Square and the 'fountain's silver weed' could be the fountains in the square, a famous spot for pigeons and starlings and there is a church – St Martin-in-the-Fields – on one side. We can be sure this is London rather than some other city because Surbiton is a London suburb.

6. Darkness fell and I left my office and set off to the bus-stop along with hundreds of others. We swept along the street like a wave, most of us pretty tired and desperate to get home after a long day's work. Once on the bus the journey took a long time because of the traffic but as we got farther away from the city centre it began to thin out – like coming to the surface after a long underwater swim. Getting home at last was peaceful and a great relief.

- Answer the question using full sentences.
- If you really don't know the answer, make a sensible guess. Say what you're doing and give your reasons, looking for clues in the poem.
- Spend time reading the poem, thinking and making notes before trying to write answers.
- If you are asked to use your imagination to continue the theme of a poem, remember that this is still a question to see if you have understood the poem. So the more you base your imaginative answer on what is in the poem, the more marks you will get.

Your turn

Now try the sample questions on page 25 for yourself and compare your answers with the sample answers above. Don't forget the tips above.

Summary

You should now know the following:

1. How to approach the poetry comprehension questions of the 13+ exam.
2. The different terms used to describe the various elements of a poem.

Test yourself

Before moving on to the next chapter, make sure you can answer the following questions. The answers are at the back of the book.

1. What is a metaphor?
2. What is a simile?
3. What is personification?
4. What is alliteration?
5. What is assonance?

Chapter 5: Reading at scholarship level

There is no single or correct way of responding to a poem or piece of prose. The important thing is that the reader comes to sensible, well-informed – sometimes imaginative – conclusions based on his or her reading of what is in the provided text.

This is particularly true at scholarship level.

5.1 Answering the reading paper at scholarship level

The Common Academic Scholarship English paper is 1 hour 45 minutes long and it is designed to challenge you. Its purpose is to give the opportunity to show how deeply and widely you can think and what you can do. It consists of two or more passages which share a theme.

The examination requires you to write about the passages, how they are written and how they are put together. You will get credit for being creative and original in the way you answer.

Below are two examples of the sorts of passages and questions you might get on your paper.

The answers which follow are merely examples of one (in each case) possible way of answering. You may have different ideas. How many marks would *you* give the sample answers and why?

Q. *Sample question*

Both these passages are about food, service and attitudes to it. The first, which is fiction, was written 154 years before the second which is personal comment by a journalist.

Extract A

Plumstead Episcopi is a village in the fictional county of Barsetshire. We are at the rectory there.

1 *And now let us observe the well-furnished breakfast-parlour at Plumstead Episcopi, and the comfortable air of all the belongings of the rectory. Comfortable they certainly were, but neither gorgeous nor grand; indeed considering the money that had been spent there, the eye and taste might have been better served; there was an air of heaviness about the rooms which might have*
5 *been avoided without any sacrifice to propriety; colours might have been better chosen and lights more perfectly diffused: but perhaps in doing so the thorough clerical aspect of the whole might have been somewhat marred; at any rate it was not without ample consideration that those thick, dark, costly carpets were put down; those embossed, but sombre papers hung up; those heavy curtains draped so as to half-exclude the light of the sun: nor were these old-fashioned chairs,*
10 *bought at a price far exceeding modern goods, without a purpose. The breakfast service on the table was equally costly and equally plain; the apparent object had been to spend money without obtaining brilliancy or splendour. The urn was thick and solid silver, as were also the tea-pot, coffee-pot, cream-ewer, and sugar-bowl; the cups were old, dim dragon china, worth about a pound a piece, but very despicable in the eyes of the uninitiated. The silver forks were so heavy*
15 *as to be disagreeable to the hand, and the bread-basket was of a weight really formidable to any but robust persons. The tea consumed was of the very best, the coffee the very blackest, the*

cream the very thickest; there was dry toast and buttered toast, muffins and crumpets; hot bread and cold bread, white bread and brown bread, home-made bread and bakers' bread, wheaten bread and oaten bread, and if there be any other breads than these, they were there; there were
20 eggs in napkins, and crispy bits of bacon under silver covers; and there were little fishes in a little box, and devilled kidneys frizzling on a hot-water dish; which by-the-by, were placed closely contiguous to the plate of the worthy archdeacon himself. Over and above this, on a snow-white napkin, spread upon the sideboard, was a huge ham and a huge sirloin; the latter having laden the dinner table on the previous evening. Such was the ordinary fare of Plumstead Episcopi.

(From *The Warden* by Anthony Trollope, 1853)

Extract B

Table Talk is a weekly column in the Sunday Times magazine.

1 *I took Giles Coren to dinner at Wild Honey, because I wanted to get some tips on how to do this job properly. I think I'm probably too codgered and crepit. I need to get down with the young'uns, learn to worry the future instead of pat the past care about how far my water has travelled.*

I'm rather in awe of Giles. He is the food critic's food critic, encompassing the shoulder-shaking
5 *humour of Matthew Fort, the modest expertise of Michael Winner, the literary pyrotechnics of Jay Rayner, and the dress sense of Charles Campion.*

He brought his utterly delightful life partner, Rachel, who was waiting with bated briefs to see if she had got a job as a lap-dancer or barrister. I couldn't quite hear which, and it's embarrassing to ask again.

10 *Wild Honey used to be Drones, originally a club owned by Marco Pierre White and then Ben Goldsmith. Neither was wholly successful. I remember the kitchen as being mean, even for a racing yacht. This time it has been taken on by the estimable team from Artubus. The menu is French-ish – more French exchange, really. The ingredients are written in Frog, but the cooking style and construction are pretty Anglo.*

15 *We started with pistou soup, which was polite but uninteresting, and young, tender leek vinaigrette. Baby leeks don't taste of much. I chose a braised pig's head with caramelised onion, which was a brick off adequate, and the calf's head with sauce gribiche, which was better, but only because two heads are better than one.*

The bavette of beef steak was cooked to be as soft as fillet. It wasn't; it was like an end of boiled
20 *rope. The point of this cut is flavour – it was underhung. Giles's Limousin veal with cavelo nero was the best choice, although the characteristic flavour of Italian winter brassica was entirely missing. In a blind tasting, I'd have guessed boiled barrister's rug before cabbage.*

Waffles for pudding were like packet breakfast. The best thing was a madeleine. It came with a so-so crème caramel. Service was chummy and attentive – and so it should be with Giles in the
25 *house. They use the service charge to make up the wages.*

The Blonde liked the food better than I did. I think the quality of the ingredients was nothing like as good as the quality of the kitchen. But that's just me. I asked Giles what I should write. He said it was all much better when he was here first time. So there you have it. Wild Honey – better if you go with Giles Coren.

(Slightly abridged from A. A. Gill's article in *The Sunday Times*, 22nd July 2007)

Q. 1. (a) From Extract A what impression do you form of the archdeacon and his breakfast parlour?

You might like to consider:

- his home
- social position
- material wealth.

(15 marks)

(b) From Extract B what impression do you form of Wild Honey?

You might like to consider:

- descriptions
- jokes
- Giles Coren.

(15 marks)

2. Compare the two extracts. In which ways are they similar? In which ways are they different? Remember that they were written in different eras for different purposes. (30 marks)

3. What impression do you get of the two writers of these extracts, Anthony Trollope and A. A. Gill? (30 marks)

(Total marks: 100 including up to 10 marks for excellence of expression and mastery of spelling, punctuation and grammar.)

A. *Sample answers*

1. (a) The archdeacon hasn't yet arrived in his breakfast parlour so we don't 'see' him. This paragraph is setting the scene. We can, however, deduce quite a bit about him from his breakfast parlour and its contents.

The 'worthy archdeacon' is wealthy. His breakfast parlour is 'well-furnished' and comfortable with 'thick dark costly carpets and expensive chairs.' 'Considering the money that had been spent there' implies that large sums of money are available and have paid for the things being described. Everything on view cost a lot of money. Trollope stresses this throughout the paragraph.

Yet it is not showy or fashionable, which tells us something about the archdeacon. 'The apparent object was to spend money without obtaining brilliancy or splendour.'

The chairs are old fashioned (antique?) and the cups are old and not attractive to most people. Even the cutlery and bread baskets are heavy. The stress is on quality.

The archdeacon clearly values food too. In his breakfast parlour everything is the best and there is plenty of it – although, of course, Trollope is using hyperbole to make a point here. He lists, for example, the different sorts of bread which are always available and the wide choice of breakfast dishes served – like a modern top-quality hotel or good restaurant. But it isn't a special occasion. The author tells us drily that this is 'the ordinary fare of Plumstead Episcopi.'

Why has someone (a servant) put the dish of devilled kidneys next to the archdeacon's plate? No doubt it is because he likes them and is in the habit of eating them for breakfast.

There is a sense that the archdeacon can afford to have exactly what he wants which means he probably has a superior social position in the village. As a clergyman living in the rectory he would have this anyway, but being well-off seems to make him more confident and sure of himself.

His breakfast parlour and, presumably, the rest of his house seems to 'make a statement' about who he is and the status he has. I imagine his money is 'old' rather than 'new.'

(b) Wild Honey is an exclusive French restaurant – probably in London – which has recently come under new management. It used to be a club and its kitchen is small. The menu is written in French but – according to this writer – the way the dishes are cooked and the atmosphere in the room are not particularly French. The waiters and waitresses are friendly and efficient.

The author went to Wild Honey to try the food with three other people – Giles Coren, Mr Coren's partner, Rachel, and someone the writer calls 'The Blonde'. They ate dinner together.

The writer does not like the food. He makes rather outrageous, exaggerated jokes about how nasty it tasted. He found his soup and his leek starter boring ('polite but uninteresting'). He compares his steak with 'an end of boiled rope' and some cabbage which is meant to be special with 'boiled barrister's rug'. The waffles he had for pudding remind him of 'packet breakfast'.

He suspects that, although the cooking is quite good, the chef is using cheap or substandard raw materials. 'I think the quality of the ingredients was nothing like as good as the quality of the kitchen.'

All of this is his personal view, however. He says that The Blonde liked the food and that Giles Coren, another, younger and much respected food critic, said it had improved since his previous visit.

2. Both extracts are about food and the way that it is presented.

Because Extract B is a restaurant review (like a book or theatre review), the journalist has a responsibility to tell his readers about the food and how it tasted in case they want to try the restaurant. The emphasis is on the food. This is very different from Extract A in which the author is using the food and the room it is in as a way of telling you more about a person. The food is there to show the reader (and, within the novel, visitors to Plumstead Episcopi) how prosperous the archdeacon is and how big he is in his community. In a sense the taste of the food doesn't matter. The emphasis is on appearance and impression.

For the same reason Extract A gives a great deal of detail about furniture, cutlery, the breakfast service and other things in the room. There is very little in Extract B about the dining area at Wild Honey.

On the other hand passage A is merely a description. There are no characters (except the archdeacon who is mentioned but not present). In contrast Passage B is full of characters. There are four at the dining table. The writer compares Giles Coren with four other people. He names the previous owners of the restaurant and he comments on the 'chummy and attentive' service – which means the people who served him. There is also conversation – as the writer tries to ask Rachel about her job and as he asks Giles Coren for his opinion of the restaurant. That makes it a much livelier piece than Passage A. This may be partly because people in the mid-nineteenth century were more willing to read detailed descriptions than most readers are now, although the two passages are from different genres. One is an extract from a novel while the other is a newspaper article.

Both passages are witty, but Passage B more obviously so. In Passage A Trollope is clearly amused by the luxury of the breakfast parlour which he describes not as if he had made it up but as if he were a visitor (such as a journalist) recording his impressions. And his final ironic comment about 'ordinary fare' is funny because obviously it wouldn't be ordinary at all in the everyday world. It's a way of showing that the archdeacon is a bit cut off from other people.

A A Gill includes so many jokes that you don't notice some of them until you look again more closely. Rachel, for example, is waiting with 'bated briefs' (a pun on 'bated breath'). The word briefs could be a lawyer's instructions or female underwear. I don't think this is particularly funny and it doesn't add much to the piece. Like Trollope, Gill ends his piece with a witticism: 'Wild Honey – better if you go with Giles Coren.'

Although their specific purposes are different, in a way both pieces are written for entertainment. Many people read newspaper reviews – not because they plan to try out what is being reviewed but because they like reading them. And novels are almost always read for pleasure. That is partly why Trollope and Gill both try to amuse. I think the Trollope extract is more successful. There's a sense in Gill's piece that he is trying to include as many jokes as he can and it gets a bit laboured.

3. A A Gill is an entertaining journalist. He knows, or knows of, many people (such as Mathew Fort, Michael Winner, Jay Rayner and Charles Campion with whom he compares

Giles Coren). Although he writes with great confidence he claims to be 'in awe of' Giles Coren who is evidently younger. By comparison, Gill refers to himself as 'codgered and crepit' (note the alliteration) and to Mr Coren as a 'young'un' willing to look forward rather than back. Gill is himself a food critic, but he is generous in his praise for Mr Coren, calling him 'the food critic's food critic.'

Anthony Trollope, on the other hand, is a novelist writing in the third person but you can feel his presence in Extract A. Someone is observing the archdeacon's breakfast parlour and making comments about it – and that person is Trollope. He describes what he 'sees' but he also makes judgements and makes his own feelings clear. He thinks it is a bit ridiculous to have twelve different sorts of bread ('and if there be any other breads than these they were there') in one room for one man and his family. And why does he need the best tea, the blackest coffee and the thickest cream? The author is laughing gently at the archdeacon's excesses, but there may be a serious point here. Back in 1853 some people in Britain would have been very poor and in need of food (there were no pensions or payments to people unable to work then). Such people must have lived in the archdeacon's fictional village. Perhaps Trollope is concerned about people like the archdeacon (a Christian clergyman) apparently not sharing more.

There is absolutely no sense of social conscience in the Gill piece. The restaurant he is describing is probably very expensive. Many people could not afford to eat in it. And in some parts of the world people can hardly afford to eat at all. But Gill's job – or what he sees as his job – is to ignore hunger and poverty and to write in detail about luxury food.

Both writers have a well-developed sense of humour. Trollope's is drier and depends on irony and understatement. Gill's is heavier and often uses elaborate puns. While Gill is very dismissive, condemning the food quite rudely, Trollope's style is more subtle. For example the cups were 'very despicable' in the eyes of anyone not versed in antiques but they cost 'a pound a piece' which would be a bit like £100 today. Trollope is poking fun at this.

As you revise, study these examples and pit yourself against the sample answers.

Ask yourself how far you agree or disagree. Practise writing what **you** would have written.

Or you might prefer to write your own answers first and then compare them with the answers given here.

Remember that, at scholarship level, there are probably as many ways of getting the marks as there are candidates for the exam.

Your turn

Now try the sample questions on page 30 for yourself and compare your answers with the sample answers above.

Q. *Sample question*

Poem A

Requiescat

1 *STREW on her roses, roses,*
And never a spray of yew.
In quiet she reposes:
Ah! would that I did too.

5 *Her mirth the world required:*
She bathed it in smiles of glee.
But her heart was tired, tired,
And now they let her be.

Her life was turning, turning,
10 *In mazes of heat and sound.*
But for peace her soul was yearning,
And now peace laps her round.

Her cabin'd, ample Spirit,
It flutter'd and fail'd for breath.
15 *To-night it doth inherit*
The vasty hall of Death.

(By Matthew Arnold (1822–1888))

Poem B

Requiescat

1 *Tread lightly, she is near*
Under the snow,
Speak gently, she can hear
The daisies grow.

5 *All her bright golden hair*
Tarnished with rust
She that was young and fair
Fallen to dust.

Lily-like, white as snow,
10 *She hardly knew*
She was a woman, so
Sweetly she grew.

Coffin-board, heavy stone,
Lie on her breast;
15 *I vex my heart alone,*

She is at rest.

Peace, peace; she cannot hear
Lyre or sonnet;
All my life's buried here,
20 *Heap earth upon it.*

(By Oscar Wilde (1854–1900))

N.B. *Requiescat* is Latin for 'May he (or she) rest.' It is often used on gravestones and memorials.

Q. 1. (a) From Poem A what impression do you get of the dead girl and the narrator's attitude to her?

You might like to consider:

- her appearance and manner
- her death
- the language used.

(20 marks)

(b) From Poem B what impression do you get of the dead girl and the narrator's attitude to her?

You might like to consider:

- her appearance and manner
- her death
- the language used.

(20 marks)

2. Compare the two poems. In what ways are they similar? In what ways are they different?

You might like to consider:

- which poem you find more convincing
- which creates a clearer image of the dead girl
- how the rhythm of the two poems compares and which one seems technically better
- which you find the more moving and why.

(30 marks)

3. What impression do you get of Oscar Wilde and Matthew Arnold from these poems? (20 marks)

(Total marks: 100 including up to 10 marks for excellence of expression and mastery of spelling, punctuation and grammar.)

A. *Sample answers*

1. (a) Mathew Arnold's 'Requiescat' presents a girl whose outward appearance was cheerful and happy ('mirth' and 'smiles of glee') but within herself she was troubled and probably ill. Her heart was 'tired tired' and the repetition here – and of 'turning' rhymed with the mournful word 'yearning' in the next verse – conveys someone who is internally and physically weary.

It is hard to tell whether her illness was mental or physical. The narrator may mean that her heart was unable to function properly so that her spirit, eventually 'flutter'd and failed for breath.' On the other hand poets often use the word 'heart' in a symbolic way to mean a person's basis of love and feeling. So did she die of a 'broken heart? If her illness was psychiatric – her life 'turning turning/In mazes of heat and sound' it is possible that she suffered from what we would now call depression or extreme stress and that she committed suicide.

She had, in life, a 'cabined, ample Spirit' which seems to suggest that she was generous, loving and enthusiastic ('ample') although she also had self-control if she was 'cabin'd'. In a way 'cabin'd' and 'ample' contradict each other. Perhaps the oxymoron stresses her confusion.

There is also a feeling in the poem that she might have loved someone who didn't return her love. The narrator wants to 'strew on her roses' and roses usually are a symbol of passion in poetry. The word 'cabin'd' reminds me of Viola in *Twelfth Night* (which we read last term). Disguised as a boy she secretly loves Orsino for a long time before he realises that he loves her too. She tells Orsino that she is 'cabin'd, cribb'd, confined, bound' and that's the only other time I have seen this word. Matthew Arnold had probably read *Twelfth Night* and might have wanted the reader to think of it too and to compare the girl in his poem with Viola.

(b) The girl in Oscar Wilde's 'Requiescat' is still a teenager ('young and fair', 'she hardly knew she was a woman') and still pure. White is the colour of purity and lilies often suggest virginity in poems. The girl is 'white as snow' and 'lily-like.' She is also 'under the snow'; so she is in a cold place where she will always be a virgin. The narrator, on the other hand, is passionate: 'I vex my heart alone.' There is no hint of how she died – just wistful description of her angelic beauty like something in an old religious painting.

The contrasts are interesting though. She had 'bright golden hair' which, now that she's dead, has lost its lustre like metal rusting. It's a gripping metaphor. She had grown up 'sweetly' too which makes the chilling 'coffin board, heavy stone' in the next line seem even more cruel.

The narrator had been in love with the girl. The implication is that he liked to court her with songs and poems ('lyre or sonnet') as if they were in a mediaeval romance. Now that she has 'fallen to dust' all his life is 'buried here.'

The girl will never grow old. Because she has died young she will remain sweet and pure forever in the narrator's mind.

2. The poems have some obvious similarities. They share a title which makes it clear that both are about death and mourning. Each is about the early death of an attractive young girl. Both are written in short-lined, four-line verses with an ABAB rhyme pattern in each. The verses are self-contained as in a ballad. There is no enjambment in either.

Both are lyric poems. It is interesting the way Wilde repeats the word 'peace' in his last verse just as Arnold repeats 'roses', 'tired' and 'turning' in his first, second and third verses. I also notice that both poems start with an imperative addressed to the reader or to some hidden listener addressed by the narrator. Had Wilde – who was 32 years younger than Arnold – read the earlier poem and been influenced by it?

Yet they are also quite different. The girl in Poem A was lively and passionate before she became ill. The narrator associates her with the warmth of roses. But death is a release for her because 'her soul was yearning.' As yew grows in churchyards and lives for a very long time it is associated with eternal life, but the narrator does not want that for this girl: '... never a spray of yew,' he writes.

In contrast, the death of the 'lily-like' girl in Poem B seems more tragic. She had not had time to enjoy life like the one in Poem A. She had barely reached adulthood and Wilde's image of her lying buried, cold and weighed down by the wood of the coffin and the stones in the earth above, is a very harsh reality.

Poem B is also – for me – more moving because the narrator is clearly devastated by her death. He longs to be buried with her because all his life is there. He invites the reader to 'heap earth upon ... ' his life. So there is a strong sense of bereavement whereas in Poem A the narrator is describing the death in a less involved way. It is sad and he is thoughtful about it but it doesn't touch him personally, although he envies her peaceful repose: 'Ah! Would that I did too'

Because poem A has four verses it is more obviously symmetrical than poem B which has five. In Poem A the repetition in the opening line of the first and third verses gives the poem a very clear pattern and divides it into two halves. I think the rhythm of Poem A is slightly more precise than in Poem B, although from a technique point of view there isn't much to choose between them.

Poem A, moreover, is religious in a way that Poem B is not. Arnold imagines the girl's 'ample' spirit being freed from her body and moving on to 'inherit/The vasty hall of death.' The word 'inherit' has connotations of acquiring something valuable. Although Arnold doesn't labour it, his 'vasty hall of death' must be some kind of heaven or after-life.

Poem B has no religious undertones. It concentrates on death as a physical end without promise. Wilde's narrator stresses the rotting ('tarnished' 'dust') of the body inside the wooden coffin, beneath the daisies, and the earth and snow.

3. Our teacher often tells us that we mustn't read poetry as if it were autobiography. So I don't think the writers of these two poems are writing about their own experiences. Just as a novelist does (for example in *Jane Eyre* by Charlotte Brontë or *Abela* by Bel Mooney) Arnold and Wilde have each created a character and tell a sort of 'story' through him. We see the character of the narrator. Arnold's speaker in Poem A longs for peace. Wilde's in Poem B is deeply distressed and can see no future for himself because the girl he idolised is dead.

It is therefore very difficult to deduce anything personal about Arnold and Wilde from these poems. The specific thing which happens to the narrator need not have happened to the poet in either case. Either writer may, of course, have experienced sadness, longing, weariness or bereavement and put a bit of the feelings involved into his poems, but we cannot assume that either has necessarily gone through the death of a young girl known to him. These poems – like fiction – have come from the imagination.

What we do learn about Arnold and Wilde is that they each had a sensitive imagination which could be channelled into quite powerful poetry. Both men were also skilled at manipulating rhyme and rhythm. Matthew Arnold's simple lines 'And now they let her be' and 'And now peace laps her round' are very beautiful, for example. He obviously saw no need to 'use a long word where a short one will do.' It's like an unaccompanied tune or song in music. Wilde seemed to prefer slightly softer sounds with adverbs, as in 'lightly', 'gently' and 'sweetly'.

Wilde's 'Requiescat' is more dramatic than Arnold's. It has more movement action and character. The speaker is mourning and lonely at the grave of the girl he loves. Oscar Wilde also wrote plays (such as 'The Importance of Being Earnest') which may explain this. I don't know what else Matthew Arnold did, but I've never heard of him as a playwright and his poem is reflective and still, rather than dramatic.

It is also possible that Arnold was more religious than Wilde because the attitude to death expressed in Poem A is more spiritual and hopeful than the cold, final separation in Poem B.

Your turn

Now try the sample questions on page 35 for yourself and compare your answers with the sample answers above.

5.2 Another way of revising for your scholarship exam

One of the most useful ways of revising is to try to get inside the head of the examiner. If you can learn to anticipate the sort of things the examiner is going to ask you, you will always be one step ahead.

- Devise your own sample papers.

Look through poetry anthologies and fiction or non-fiction books you are reading (or have read), magazines, newspapers and any other written material to which you have access.

- Take a poem which you already know well and search for another on the same theme.

Either way, find extracts and/or poems which fit together in some way.

- Then write the sort of questions based on them which you think an examiner would ask.

Now practise writing answers to your own questions – or swap with someone else.

Summary

You should now know the following:

1. How to approach the comprehension questions in the scholarship exam, for both poetry and prose.
2. How to devise your own sample papers to help with revision.

Chapter 6: Writing

Writing is a skill which you will need to master, whether you are taking exams at 11+ or 13+. In this chapter we look at the skills you need to work on.

6.1 11+ Composition

11+

If you are taking the 11+ Common Entrance examinations your composition paper will last 40 minutes (plus 5 minutes' reading and planning time). It carries 25 marks.

It gives you a choice of subjects to write about. The paper usually includes options such as:

- a story
- a piece of factual writing or personal description
- writing in which you state your views
- a review of a book – which could be poetry or a play – you have read
- a photograph or picture to use as a starting point.

You must choose **one** of these.

The examiner wants to see how well you can:

- organise your ideas in writing
- convey your opinions and ideas
- spell
- use grammar.

6.2 13+ Writing

13+

The 13+ writing paper lasts 1 hour 20 minutes (which includes planning time). It carries 50 marks.

There are **two** tasks, each worth 25 marks.

In Section A you choose one question on a book or books you have studied. There will be four to choose from – two on a set theme and two which allow you to use any book you have studied.

In Section B you must choose one question out of six. As at 11+, these can be an account of an experience, a description, a letter or diary entry, a story, or something in which you state your own or someone else's views.

The aim is to give you the opportunity to show how well you can write in different ways. It is important that you:

- write in an appropriate way for the task you have chosen
- spell correctly
- punctuate and use grammar properly
- use exciting vocabulary accurately.

6.3 A note about themes

13+

Some schools choose to organise their Year 7 and 8 English literature teaching around themes set by the Independent Schools Examinations Board.

This means that the books, plays and poetry you have studied will be linked to a theme rather than chosen at random.

If your school has used the themes, you can use that work to answer one of the theme-related questions on the 13+ writing paper.

But if your teachers have chosen not to do this, then use the books you have studied to answer one of the other two questions.

These are the themes which are set for three school years before they change. After 2015/16 the pattern will begin again with relationships:

- 2007/8, 2008/9 and 2009/10: Relationships
- 2010/11, 2011/12 and 2012/13: Conflict
- 2013/14, 2014/15 and 2015/16: Heroes or Heroines

Do not try to write too much. Make sure you leave yourself at least 5 minutes at the end to check your work. You will get more marks for writing something fairly short but accurate than you will for a longer piece of writing which is full of errors.

6.4 General advice about writing well

Whether you are at 11+, 13+ or scholarship level there are ways in which you can improve the quality of your writing.

Sentence length

Vary the length of your sentences. A piece of writing in which all the sentences are roughly the same length is usually dull and flat.

Look at an example of a professional writer using sentences of different lengths:

> *Her beauty silenced us. Despite Kenji's enthusiasm earlier, I was quite unprepared for it. I thought then that I understood Lady Maruyana's suffering: at least part of it had to be jealousy. How could any man refuse the possession of such beauty?*

(From *Across the Nightingale Floor* by Lian Hearn, 2002)

In one paragraph Lian Hearn has a sequence of sentences which have – in order – 4, 10, 18 and 10 words. Read it aloud. You will notice that varied sentence length creates rhythm which matters as much in prose as in poetry.

A useful technique is sometimes to build a paragraph of three sentences, each one shorter than the one before. It is quite dramatic and makes your reader want to hurry on to the next paragraph. Here are two examples of professional writers using it:

> *Becky knew her tirade had gone too far, that she'd spoiled the day, that it would make her mother cry, and that she'd hate herself later for making her unhappy again. But to her surprise, her mother didn't cry this time. Instead she went very quiet.*
>
> (From *Best Mate* by Michael Morpurgo, 2007)

> *Something stirred in the study window and a glow of light shone out for moment. She remembered what she had to do and tapped on the glass door. It opened almost at once.*
>
> (From *Northern Lights* by Philip Pullman, 1995)

As you revise, try writing paragraphs with sentences of different lengths. Look out for sentences of different lengths while you're reading too.

Sentence shape

Make sure that you use a variety of **shapes** for your sentences too. If you are writing a story about Adam don't start the first five sentences with Adam or 'he' followed by a verb.

Instead:

Start sometimes with a fronted clause or phrase ('Knowing that he was already late, Adam …'; 'Desperate and angry, Adam …').

Write an occasional 'inside out' sentence such as 'Because he knew Julia was in terrible danger, Adam ran as fast as he could.' (Rather than 'Adam ran as fast as he could because Julia was in terrible danger.')

If you're writing conversation, vary the position of the words which explain who is speaking. They can go at the beginning, in the middle or at the end of spoken words. Change the order of them too. Use 'Martha said' as well as 'said Martha':

> Freddy said, 'I don't believe a word of it. It just can't be true.'
>
> 'I don't believe a word of it. It just can't be true,' said Freddy.
>
> 'I don't believe a word of it,' said Freddy. 'It just can't be true.'

Stir some indirect speech into the mix of conversation too:

> Freddy said he didn't believe a word of it because it just couldn't be true.

Start some sentences with adverbs such as 'hurriedly', 'anxiously', 'now' or 'there'. For example:

> 'There, in the garden, Felicity waited.'
>
> 'Hurriedly, he leapt on his bike and began to pedal.'

Experiment occasionally with putting the verb before the subject in some of your sentences. For example: 'Suddenly, up jumped the dog.' 'Downhill marched the group towards the village.'

Study this example of a professional writer varying the shape of her sentences:

> *Uncle Acquila lived on the extreme edge of Calleva. One reached his house down a narrow side street that turned off not far from the East Gate, leaving behind the forum and the temples, and coming to a quiet angle of the old British earthworks – for Calleva had been a British Dun before it became a Roman city – where the hawthorn and hazel still grew and the shyer woodland birds still came. It was much like the other houses of Calleva, timbered and red-roofed and comfortable, built round three sides of a tiny courtyard that was smoothly turfed and set about with imported roses and gum-cistus growing in tall stone jars. But it had one peculiarity: a squat, square, flat-roofed tower rising from one corner: for Uncle Acquila. Having lived most of his life in the shadow of watch-towers from Memphis to Segedunum, he could not be comfortable without one.*

(From *The Eagle of the Ninth* by Rosemary Sutcliff, 1954)

Rosemary Sutcliff uses compound and complex sentences (interspersed with simple ones like the one which opens her paragraph) and often punctuates them with colons and semi-colons.

As you revise, practise writing paragraphs consisting of sentences of different shapes. Notice and think about sentence shape while you're reading too.

Strong verbs and nouns

It is not usually good style to clutter up your writing with too many adjectives and adverbs.

Choose strong and appropriate verbs and nouns.

Use adverbs and adjectives only if they are really necessary or add something.

For example:

> 'The water <u>trickled</u> along the <u>gully</u>' is a much better sentence than 'A *small* amount of water ran *slowly* along the bottom of the *steep little* valley.'
>
> '<u>Musicologists</u> have found the <u>manuscript</u> of one of Beethoven's <u>overtures</u> in an <u>attic</u> in Vienna.' is a much better sentence than '*Music* experts have found Beethoven's *original handwritten* copy of one of his *short* pieces in a *top-floor* room in Vienna.'

(Strong, appropriate nouns and verbs are underlined. Avoidable adjectives and adverbs are in italics.)

Using strong verbs and nouns will usually help you to create shorter sentences (see above) too.

Avoid useless adjectives and adverbs

Putting in an adjective or adverb which adds nothing can sometimes weaken a strong verb or noun. For example:

> 'I am exhausted' is stronger and clearer than 'I am really exhausted.'
>
> 'He apologised' carries more weight than 'He apologised very sincerely.'

If you feel tempted to use the adverb 'actually', or the adjective 'actual', ask yourself if you really need it. Try your sentence without it. You may be surprised how well it works when it is free of these 'clutter words'.

Avoid tautology

Overuse of adjectives and adverbs often leads to tautology – unnecessary repetition.

Do not, for example, write 'return back'. Return means to go or to give back so the adverb 'back' is tautologous.

Ascend means to go up. So never write 'ascend up'. Reply means to speak or write back so 'reply back' is an error.

As you revise, make your own list of common tautologous mistakes to avoid.

Now, for practice, work out what is wrong with this sentence recently seen in a newspaper:

> 'President Chen says the government of Taiwan plans to re-apply for UN membership again in the future.'

Paragraphing

A paragraph is, of course, a group of sentences or a subsection within a piece of prose writing (i.e. not poetry or a play).

Begin a new paragraph when:

- you introduce a new topic, idea, character or opinion
- a new person speaks in a passage of dialogue in a story
- you want dramatic effect.

Remember:

- in modern writing long, wandering paragraphs are generally regarded as weak style (although nineteenth century writers such as Jane Austen and Charles Dickens loved them)
- three or four sentences is usually an ideal paragraph length
- if in doubt, begin a new paragraph
- a one-sentence paragraph can be a useful way of making your writing dramatic.

Plan your writing

- ALWAYS plan prose writing of all sorts in paragraphs at the beginning of the exam.
- But when you come to write the story/essay/account – or whatever you have chosen to write – you will probably want to subdivide your paragraphs to make them shorter.

Good paragraphing shows the examiner that you can organise your ideas in writing – which is one of the main things looked for in this exam.

Avoid repetition

Apart from words like 'and' and 'the', try not to repeat words in your writing more than you can help.

Look at this example:

> *At moonrise I walked on, not ceasing until I at last reached the foot of the Black Mountains. Here I settled, and chewed upon more of Dahtet's dried meat. Then I lay upon the dusty ground that I might refresh my body with some little sleep. Across the flat land Golahka would come at dawn, and this time I knew he would cross swiftly meaning to reach our camp before I did.*
>
> (From *Apache* by Tanya Landman, 2007)

The writer uses 'cross' to avoid repeating 'walked' or 'walk'. 'Ceasing' 'settled' and 'lay' all have a sense of stopping to rest but there is no repetition.

The better your vocabulary the easier you will find it to do this.

As any teacher will tell you, a good personal word bank comes from reading widely so make sure you read as many books as you can while you are revising.

If you're writing about people try not to repeat their names more often than necessary. Of course you can use pronouns such as 'he', 'she' or 'they' but take care that it's clear exactly to whom they refer.

For occasional variety use words and phrases to refer to your characters such as:

- the boy/girl/man/woman
- the pupil/child/student
- the teacher (or any other occupation such as lorry driver, solicitor, etc.)
- her/his friend
- our neighbour.

6.5 General advice on writing a story

Plan your story

Plan your story so that you know where it's going. Never try, in an exam, to make up a story as you go along.

Q. *Sample question*

Q. Write a story which begins with a telephone conversation.

A. *Sample answer*

Your outline plan might look like this:

1. Mother and TV presenter talking on the phone. Competition results. Child has won trip to Antarctica.
2. Mother off phone – her feelings.
3. Child home from school and father from work. Mother tells them the news.
4. Flashback to advertisement for the competition and entering for it. Child's very strong ambition to see Antarctica.
5. Family discussion about which adult (mother, father or a grandparent?) will accompany the child.
6. Some time later. Setting off for the trip – airport. Meeting rest of group. Excitement.

Once you have an outline plan of your story (spend about 5 minutes creating it) you can fill in the details as you write.

Decide, for example, whether the child is a boy or a girl, how old and give him or her name. What did entering the competition involve? You might also want to provide a reason for the keenness on Antarctica. Has he or she read a lot about it or seen television documentaries? Or perhaps a great-great-grandparent was an explorer?

Your turn

Now try the sample question above for yourself (which was one of the choices on the 2007 13+ paper) using the plan given or devise a completely different plan of your own. Allow yourself about 35 minutes' writing time.

Beginnings, middles and endings

Think for a moment about any traditional fairy story.

It begins 'Once upon a time …' and it ends 'And they all lived happily ever after.' Anything which happens between these is the middle of the story.

Your story will, almost certainly, be more complex than a fairy story, but the examiner is still looking for an effective opening and a rounded-off end. Think of these as the frame which encloses your story.

Beginnings

There are many ways of starting a story. For example you can:

- Introduce a character (for example: 'Fergus was sitting on the sea wall idly drumming his heels ...').
- Set the scene (for example: 'The bell rang and Year 6 erupted noisily though the damp, grey walled area into the panelled hall where hot chocolate and buns awaited them ...').
- Describe a situation in which everything is not quite what it seems to tantalise your reader. Then in the next paragraph you explain what is really happening (for example: 'They were being attacked on all sides. The noise rattled over their heads. Adrenaline had never been higher. This was life and death ... James and Abdullah had always loved football. It was what cemented their friendship ...').
- Jump straight into unexplained dialogue and later explain who is speaking and why (for example: '"Let's go inside and find out." "Do you really think we should?" "Yes, come on." Hannah and Jessica were standing outside Horniman's Museum in London. Hannah was insisting that one of the exhibits was a famous stuffed walrus. Jessica was sceptical.').
- Make a mysterious statement to make the reader read on (for example: 'It was all Shakespeare's fault ...' or 'I have always adored apricot jam ...').

Endings

You can end in different ways too. For instance you might:

- Spring a surprise. End with something the reader was not expecting. For example, if two characters have been exploring a cave your reader is probably waiting for them to discover something interesting and come out safe at the end. Instead you could drown them as the tide comes in. If you write a love story you might end with the two people separating without the obvious 'happy ever after' ending.
- Take your characters back to where they started. So, for example, Fergus is sitting on the sea wall at the end of the story as he was at the beginning.
- End with a joke (for example: 'The moral of this story is that parents are better news than you might think.' or 'And so, you see, it isn't usually a good idea to pit yourself against a challenge – whatever teachers, pushy parents and youth leaders might tell you.').

Endings to avoid

Avoid the following:

- The narrator waking up at the end and revealing it was all a dream. (It has been done far too often before and will make the examiner sigh in exasperation.)

- Revealing that the mystery character sighted earlier (perhaps on a roadside) is the ghost of someone who died there a while ago. (This, too, is very unoriginal.)
- Tailing off without a definite ending and leaving the reader to guess.

Strong beginnings and endings almost always mean a well-written, gripping story likely to attract high marks in an examination.

Start in the middle

Some people find it very difficult to write a complete story in just over half an hour. Indeed, many an adult professional writer would find it almost impossible.

Another way of tackling the task is to imagine that you are writing two or three pages from the *middle* of an exciting, gripping, interesting or moving book. This means you don't have to worry so much about balanced and satisfying beginnings and endings. You can concentrate instead on making your writing as lively as possible.

If you do this in your exam:

- plan your writing just as carefully as if you were producing a complete story
- state clearly at the top that this is a passage extracted from an imaginary book
- give your imagined novel a title
- write a one or two sentence introduction at the top similar to the explanations teachers and examiners put in front of passages taken from books for comprehension work
- try to end on an exciting 'cliff hanger' to tantalise the reader.

Use either first or third person

Most stories are told:

- by an invisible narrator who describes from the outside what is happening to characters and refers to them as he, she or they – known grammatically as the third person
- by a character who is part of the story him or herself so there is an 'I' – or first person – in the story
- by more than one first person narrator (quite common in novels – such as *The Woman in White* by Wilkie Collins, 1860 or *The Boleyn Inheritance* by Philippa Gregory, 2006) but rarely appropriate in a short story unless it takes the form of a series of short letters
- by a mixture of first and third person narrators (as in some modern novels but not, usually, in short stories).

- Any story you write in your exam will be quite short so use either the first person or the third person.
- Even if you opt for the third person you are quite likely to present what happens through the eyes of one character.
- The important thing is to make up your mind at the beginning who is telling your story. Stick to it. Stories which begin in third person and then slip into the first by mistake go badly wrong and lose many marks.

Characters and dialogue

There are some key points to remember when considering your characters and the dialogue within your composition.

Create vivid and interesting characters

Create some vivid and interesting characters for your story, but do not try to include too many. Although some novels have dozens of characters, the sort of story you will have time to write in your exam is very short. You do not have space for more than two or three main characters. If you try to include more, your story will be confused and confusing.

Use detail

Present each character in as much detail as you can. Show him or her doing and saying things as a way of communicating to your reader what a character is like. This is usually more effective than just telling the reader what someone is like.

So rather than writing 'Sophie is an intelligent girl who loves books', show her curled up with *David Copperfield* by Charles Dickens. Rather than informing the reader that Jake's grandmother is very well off, show him getting a £500 cheque from her for his birthday.

Use dialogue

Use dialogue to show what characters are like too. Let them introduce themselves to your reader through what they say. This is much more like real life and works well in stories.

Learn **SCIA** (**S**how **C**haracters **i**n **A**ction) and keep it in mind as you write your story.

Vary words of speaking

When you are writing dialogue try to make it more interesting and less repetitive by using words other than 'said' to explain who is speaking. There are many other possibilities, some of them quite colourful, such as:

whispered	bellowed	demanded	questioned
murmured	muttered	asked	breathed
enquired	exclaimed	declaimed	suggested
proposed	shouted	mumbled	grumbled
growled	groaned		

> As part of your revision, create a list of your own words to use when you are writing dialogue. Watch out for examples in your reading.

Keep the dialogue flowing

Make dialogue as punchy as you can. Sometimes, if two characters are speaking alternately in short sentences, you don't need explanatory words to tell the reader who is speaking. This has the effect of making the dialogue run very fast down the page and is good, for example, for arguments.

Make names believable

Give the characters in your story believable names. In real life a person's name is usually related to:

- The period in which he or she was born. In the early 20th century many babies were given names such Albert, Doris, Phyllis and Vera. In the middle of the 20th century Susan, David, Peter and Anne were popular. By the 1990s, it was Oliver, Chloe, Charlotte and Ben. Some names, of course, move in and out of fashion. Old names such as George, Henry, Florence and Beatrice are popular again now. So are names which used to be surnames such as Scott, Lucas and Lee.
- The country he or she comes from. Names such as Callum and Douglas are often Scottish. Huw and Gwyneth are Welsh names. Names such as Eva, Elena and Nicolas (spelled without the 'h') are popular in many European countries.
- His or her social class. In the early 20th century someone called Violet was more likely (although of course there were exceptions) to be a servant than a girl named Alexandra. A boy named Ron was more likely to work in, say, a coalmine, than a young man named Julian.

> Your story will ring much truer if you give your characters appropriate names. Think about the names of the people you know – the very elderly, the middle-aged, younger people and anyone you know who comes (or whose family comes) from outside Britain.

6.6 General advice on writing a factual account or description

You might choose a writing task of this sort:

- Write a detailed description of a place which you have visited on holiday.
- Write a detailed description of a lonely place which has made a strong impression on you.
- Write in detail about someone known to you or your family who is unusual or eccentric.
- Describe an occasion when you were worried or in danger.

Or you might choose, from the options on the examination paper, a 'flexible' title which can be treated in any way and use it as the basis for a factual account or description.

For example, one of the writing choices on the 2007 13+ writing paper was 'The Voice'. This could, of course, have been written as a story. But it could also have been the basis for a factual or descriptive account, say, of how you or someone known to you has used your/his/her voice in singing or drama, the lessons, performances and so on. Or it could have been a real-life account of a particular voice you have heard and been impressed by, perhaps in a concert.

Q. *Sample question*

As a revision exercise, choose one of the ideas above – or invent a similar one of your own – and practise with it. Make sure you spend at least 5 minutes planning it and making notes. Work it out in paragraphs but be prepared to sub-divide these as you write. Allow yourself about 35 minutes' writing time. Make sure you check your spelling, punctuation and expression carefully before your time is up.

In a factual account or description:

- **Begin strongly.** Begin with a strong statement which will make your reader want to read on. For example: 'My Uncle Joe is a puppeteer.' Or 'Everyone in my family has childhood memories of Bournemouth since my great great grandfather bought a holiday home there in 1921.' Or 'I was in the water. It was deep and cold. I was fully dressed. There was no one in sight.'
- **Use your senses.** Mention sights, sounds, smells, tastes and the feel of things. Use all five senses to bring your writing to life.
- **Use your memories.** Use your memories and make them as entertaining as you can.
- **Don't use unnecessary words.** Remember not to 'spice' your description by using extra adverbs (such as seriously, very and extremely) and adjectives which don't really add anything. As for other forms of writing, choose precise verbs and nouns instead.
- **Use metaphors and similes.** Use interesting – and original – metaphors and similes.

6.7 General advice on writing your opinions

Examiners often invite you to write your views on something people disagree about.

For example:

- There has been much debate about what children should and should not eat as a regular part of their diet. What are your own thoughts on this subject?
- Fox hunting has been banned in England. What are your views about this?
- *TV rots the senses in the head!*
  It kills the imagination dead!
  It clogs and clutters up the mind!
  It makes the child so dull and blind!

  (From *Charlie and the Chocolate Factory* by Roald Dahl)

  Do you agree? What are your own thoughts on the subject of television?

Make your case

- Your job is to set down what you think and to explain why.
- When you are planning your writing, note any evidence you can think of to support your views. It might, for example, be from your own experience, things you have read or heard in the media (such as newspapers, television or the internet), information you have been given by your teachers or parents, or anything you have noticed or learned from other sources.

For example, if you are writing about healthy eating, you might mention children you know who eat unusually healthily or unhealthily, facts and figures (if you know them) about children becoming less healthy and fatter because of the food many of them eat, and differences parents and schools can make, with examples. Or, if you are arguing that there is nothing wrong with children's diets, then mention some supporting evidence to prove your points. And/or you might decide to mention your views about the responsibility adults have towards children's eating and whether or not most of them set a good example. If so, again, you will need some evidence.

Start with an anecdote

A piece of opinion writing often works well if you start with an anecdote (a little story about something which has happened to you or someone you know, or something you saw). Then widen out your argument with evidence and end with a comment which links the evidence to your anecdote.

> Many newspaper columnists often use the formula of an anecdote followed by evidence. Read as many as you can – particularly in the weekend newspapers – as part of your revision.

Plan your points

List in your plan the points you want to make. As you write you will probably want to subdivide these into shorter paragraphs.

Useful words and phrases for opinion essays:

- I contend/believe/think/suggest/propose/insist ...
- Take ... (at the beginning of a sentence to introduce an example)
- What is more ...
- Moreover ...
- Nevertheless/nonetheless ...
- I would argue ...
- Evidence suggests ...
- Historically/traditionally ...
- In the past ...
- Some people think ...
- I wonder ...

6.8 11+ Writing a book-related composition

11+

One of the writing options on the 11+ composition paper invites you to write about a book you have read.

You may base your answer on any book you have read in or out of school – and it can be a poetry book or play text as well as any kind of fiction or non-fiction book. The question is always a general one which doesn't specify any particular books. This is so that you can answer it with reference to any book you wish.

At the top of your answer always write the title and author of the book you have chosen to write about.

You may be asked briefly to summarise 'your' book or part of it. Or the question might ask you for your views on the book, its plot; or a character or episode which you found particularly striking.

Express, compare, state

You will always get higher marks if you:

- Express your opinions rather than use too much of your space/time simply retelling the story or describing what the book is about.

- Compare the book with other books or, for example, its character with characters from other books. (For example, 'Tom from *Goodnight Mr Tom* is rather like Silas in *Silas Marner*. Each is a lonely old man who comes to life when a child comes to live with him.')
- State your preferences and give reasons for them.

Don't be afraid to write in your exam about a book you did **not** enjoy. As long as you give reasons for your views and preference you can still get high marks.

In general, it is probably safer to choose a book you have studied in school rather than one you have read individually at home. If you have worked on it as a class text, your teacher will have helped you to learn more about it. You will have taken part in class discussions and you have probably already done some written work connected with the book as part of your class work. You will, therefore, find it easier to write thoughtfully about it in your exam than if you try to write about something you have read casually and quickly on your own.

Stick to the book

In a book review try to avoid phrases and statements which don't refer to what is in the book. For example, none of the following adds much:

- This is a wonderful book and I have recommended it to all my friends.
- I give this great book five stars.
- I shall never forget this book.
- I couldn't put this book down.
- It's a great page-turner.
- This is the best book I have ever read.
- My mum and dad both think it is a good book too.
- A great book for all ages.

Remember that in an exam you are not trying to 'sell' the book to your reader. Rather, you are trying to show him or her how thoughtfully you have read it and how well you can communicate your ideas about it in writing.

Use content

Think of the content of the book as evidence. Use it and refer to it to support the points you make.

Useful phrases and statements for book-related compositions:

- X is the best of the three books by Y I have read because …
- B, with its ——, —— plot and ——, —— characters, is …

- I enjoyed/admired the episode in which —— because ...
- The characters are ...
- The plot is ...
- This book is better than —— because ...

Don't be vague

Avoid vague words like 'good', 'great' and 'wonderful'. Instead use specific words such as 'strong', 'powerful' or 'menacing' to describe characters, or 'twisted', 'satisfying', 'puzzling' or 'well constructed' to describe a plot. If it's a non-fiction book use words like 'informative', 'provocative', 'detailed'.

Refer to the author

Refer to the author and what he or she is doing as much as you can. Below are some verbs and phrases to help you to do that.

The author ...

- presents
- wants us to see that
- leads us to think that
- gives us
- offers us
- seems to think
- has a habit of

Look particularly at how the author uses dialogue. What does it add to the story? What does it tell about the characters?

Q. *Sample question*

Part of your revision could be to plan and write, for practice, an examination answer relating to any book you have read in class this school year. Spend 5 minutes planning. Limit your writing time to 30 minutes. Take 5 minutes at the end to check your work carefully.

Q. Write about any book you have read recently. Explain in detail what you thought of it and why.

6.9 13+ Response to studied literature

13+

This is a compulsory section of the 13+ writing paper.

There will be four questions on the paper. You must choose one.

Your school may have decided to use the set English Literature theme which changes every three years (see page 41). Two of the four questions set will be related to this. The other two can be answered with reference to **any** book or books you have studied.

Like the book-related 11+ questions, the 13+ literature questions are general. They do not mention specific books.

The examiner particularly wants you to write about moments of drama, change, development, contrast and other things which you find interesting in the book or books you have chosen to write about.

The response to the studied literature question is worth 25 marks. You should spend a total of about 40 minutes (half of the whole paper) on it.

Use 5 minutes to plan and make notes. Spend 30 minutes writing. Leave 5 minutes at the end to check your work thoroughly.

You will get marks for expressing your opinions and preferences – with reasons – and for making comparisons.

As always, you will also get a higher mark if you write in good, appropriate English with correct spelling, punctuation and grammar.

Retelling the story in your own words is never the answer to the question.

Hints for higher marks

If you want to get higher marks, think about the following.

Write what the question asks for

Do not simply retell the story of the book you have decided to write about. If the question is about self-sacrifice and heroism, plan your answer fully and write about that. If it is about how much characters change then pick a couple of examples and make sure you use the word change (or transition, transformation, development and other synonyms) in every paragraph.

Make comparisons

You will always get credit for making comparisons. So, even if you do this in only half a sentence, try to compare your subject with something else from another book. For example, in an essay about suffering in *To Kill a Mockingbird* you might write 'Like Jane in *Jane Eyre*, Scout, the narrator of *To Kill a Mockingbird*, looks back on childhood and conveys a strong sense of the suffering and learning that she had to work through.' If you are writing about heroism in *The*

Pearl you could say: 'Kino in *The Pearl* develops and learns as much as George in *Of Mice and Men* by the same author.' You can also, of course, compare characters and situations within the same book.

Mention the author

Don't forget that characters are created by authors. Mention the author's name at least once in every paragraph. Use statements such as 'John Steinbeck never lets us forget that Lennie is dependent on George' or 'It is part of Harper Lee's storytelling technique that we see everything through the eyes of an adult looking back at herself as a child.' Use appropriate vocabulary. Words such as plot, characterisation, narrative shape, dialogue and first person narrative are useful.

> During the revision period you should re-read the two or three books you have studied recently and which you are likely to write about in the exam so that they are fresh in your mind. Remind yourself of any written work you have done on them or notes you have made too.

Useful verbs for writing about literature

The author ...

evokes	argues	hints that	characterises
gives us	conveys	implies	shows
intends	pretends	means	communicates
describes	depicts	criticises	builds up
imagines			

> As you revise, add words of your own to this list.

Q. *Sample question*

Often characters develop and learn as a result of their experiences during the course of a story. Choose one text you have studied and consider to what extent the main character learns and changes as the story unfolds.

Write a practice, timed answer, to this question.

If you have time write a second answer to this question referring to a different book.

Summary

You should now know the following:

1. How to approach the writing paper of the 11+ exam.
2. How to approach the writing paper of the 13+ exam.

3. How to use sentences of different length and shape in your writing.
4. How to choose strong verbs and nouns so as not to clutter your writing.
5. How to use paragraphs well so that you can organise your ideas.
6. How to plan your writing.
7. How to create characters and dialogue.
8. How to write a factual account or your opinion.
9. How to write about a book you have read.

Test yourself

Before moving on to the next chapter, make sure you can answer the following questions. Suggested answers are at the back of the book.

1. Amend the following sentences so that the length is varied, using suitable connecting words and pronouns:

   (a) Liam stretched. Liam yawned. Liam got out of bed.

   (b) Michelle ran to the newsagents. Michelle opened the door wide. Michelle gasped as she looked inside.

2. Remove the unnecessary adverbs and adjectives from the following sentences to create strong sentences:

   (a) 'Actually that sounds absolutely fantastic!' I shouted loudly with extreme delight.

   (b) It sounded really great as she explained the specific detail of her new plan.

3. Remove the tautologous words in the following sentences:

   (a) They descended down the path in succession one after the other.

   (b) The unmarried young bachelor couldn't wait to meet the girl of his dreams.

Chapter 7: Using English accurately

As well as reading carefully, writing perceptive answers and producing imaginative essays, you need to show in your English exam papers that you can write with precision. That means paying close attention to grammar, punctuation and spelling.

Usually these are not marked separately – although some senior schools choose to give a separate mark out of 10 for grammar and spelling. This means that if you write imaginatively and have a good vocabulary but have, for example, a spelling learning difficulty the examiner will give you the marks you deserve for your ideas without being put off by your spelling.

In most cases, however, your grammar, punctuation and spelling are marked along with the content you write. It is part of the general impression your work gives the examiner – and an important part. So it is essential that you revise the technicalities of English thoroughly so that you make as few mistakes as possible in your writing. Errors will cost you marks.

You will not be asked specific questions about grammar in your paper. But there are at least two good reasons for knowing the main word classes:

- If you have good background knowledge of the shape of sentences and the different sorts of words which go into a good one you are more likely to write well.
- It can be useful to use the vocabulary of grammar in a comprehension answer. You might write for example: 'The poet's use of aggressive verbs …' or 'the effect of the author's list of abstract nouns suggests …'

7.1 Word classes or 'parts of speech'

Here is a brief summary of the parts of speech and how they work. There is more detail – if you need it – in *So you really want to learn English* Books 1, 2 and 3.

Remember that words are not loyal. They belong to different groups depending on the job they are required to do in a particular sentence. So concentrate on what sort of a word it is in the sentence you are writing or studying. Don't worry about what sort of word it might be in a different context.

- Try to revise one of these eight parts of speech each day.
- Make up more examples of your own as part of your revision.
- Tick each off when you are sure you have learned it.

Nouns

A noun is a naming word. There are several sorts.

- Common – for example: table, book, house, boy
- Proper – for example: Manchester, Prince William, Pizza Express, River Tyne

- Abstract – for example: adoration, anger, thirst, carelessness
- Collective – for example: herd (of cattle), pack (of cards), flock (of birds or sheep)

Verbs

A verb is the action or 'being' word which shows you what is happening in a sentence.

- We **walked** all the way to town.
- Mr Smith **is** our teacher.
- '**Run** faster!' **shouted** the cricket coach.
- We **are** the champions.

Verbs can be expressed in various versions of the past, present and future tenses, depending on when the action or situation took, takes or will take place.

In sentences verbs often consist of several words because they sometimes use auxiliary (helping) verbs – to have or to be – to show the tense.

- In October we **shall have been living** in our house for ten years.
- I **was wandering** along the corridor.
- You **will be** late for school.
- **Has** she **been reading** *Tom's Midnight Garden?*

Adjectives

Adjectives are describing words which 'qualify' or 'modify' – or tell you more about – nouns.

- I love **hot**, **sunny summer** days.
- Drink your tea before it gets **cold**.
- **Red** roses are my **favourite** flowers.

They can be used in a comparative (more) form:

- hotter, more exciting, better

Or a superlative (most) form:

- hottest, most exciting, best

Adverbs

Adverbs are describing words which 'qualify' or 'modify' – or tell you more about – verbs. They usually tell you how, when, where or why something happens. If it helps, think of **adverbs** as words which **add** to the meaning of **verbs.**

Think of an adverb as an add-verb because it adds to the meaning of the verb but be careful to spell **adverb** correctly.

- Oliver Twist and his friends ate **hungrily**.
- My horse **rapidly** overtook hers.
- Let's do it **now**.
- Snow lay **everywhere**.

Adverbs also sometimes qualify other adverbs or adjectives.

- The girl was **unusually** small.
- We thought it was best to get there **quite** quickly

Pronouns

Pronouns stand in the place of nouns. They mean you don't have to keep clumsily repeating the nouns in your sentences. There are several sorts.

- Personal (when it's the subject of the verb) – I, he, she, we, they, it. For example: '**He** and **I** went swimming.'
- Personal (when it's the object or 'receiver' of the verb) – him, her, us, them. For example: 'Mrs Wentworth told **us** what to do.'
- Demonstrative – this dog, that pencil. Such pronouns often drop the accompanying noun. For example: 'This is my idea' (not 'This idea is my idea') or 'This is mine' (not 'This glass/pencil/bag is mine').
- Possessive – his, her, hers, mine, my, their, theirs, our, ours. For example: 'This is **his** book.' 'This book is **his**.' 'That is **our** house.' 'That house is **ours**.'
- Relative – who, which, whom, whose. For example: 'My cousin, **whom** you don't know, lives in Cornwall' or 'This is the book **which** I was telling you about.' In these examples the pronoun stands for 'my cousin' and 'the book.'

Take particular care with 'who' and 'whom'.

Whom is used when it is standing as the object of a verb or when it follows prepositions (for example to, by, of, through, from, by, at).

We use it in English when, in a differently structured variation of the sentence, we would use him (not he).

For example:

- This is the man **whom** my sister loves. (She loves **him**.)
- This is the teacher from **whom** I learned French last year. (I learnt it from **him**.)

- This is the boy with **whom** I went on a Scout camp. (I went with **him**.)
- To **whom** does this pencil case belong? (Does it belong to **him**?)

Who is used when it is standing as the subject of the verb. We use who when, in other circumstances, we would say 'he'.

For example:

- This is the man **who** loves my sister. (**He** loves her.)
- This is the teacher **who** taught me French last year. (**He** taught me.)
- This is the boy **who** went with me on a Scout camp. (**He** went with me.)
- **Who** owns this pencil case? (**He** owns it.)

Prepositions

Prepositions tell you the **position** of something in relation to something else. Think of them, if it helps, as place words (p for place and p for preposition).

- The jam is **in** the cupboard.
- **Under** the apple tree Felix is asleep.
- The dish ran away **with** the spoon.

Other prepositions include: within, inside, outside, over, beneath, above, around, up, down, into, with, at. But many of these words can, as so often in English, also be used to do other jobs in sentences when they are not being prepositions.

Conjunctions

Conjunctions are joining words. Think of the **junction** on a railway where two or more lines join.

They can be used to join short sentences to create longer ones or sometimes to hook words together.

Common everyday conjunctions include: and, or, because, as, although, but, though, so.

For example:

- The prize went jointly to Marina **and** Oliver.
- I am going fishing at the weekend **because** it is my favourite activity. (I am going fishing at the weekend. It is my favourite activity.)

Q. Write a number of short sentences (which follow on logically from each other). Then join them all up into one long sentence, using conjunctions. For example:

I don't like broccoli. I eat it. It's good for me.

There are several ways you could organise this into one long sentence. Try it for practice.

Like prepositions, conjunctions are slippery little words. The same words often get into sentences doing other jobs. Look, as ever, at **how** they are used before you decide what they are.

Articles

'The' is the definite article and refers to something specific (for example: **the** government or **the** sea refers to a specific one).

'A' is the indefinite article (for example: **a** fox or **a** poem – not specific because we are referring to any fox or poem).

'An' is a form of the indefinite article used when the next word begins with a vowel (for example: an elephant, an apple, an old coat).

Before we leave the parts of speech try, as a revision exercise, using some of the slipperiest words as different parts of speech in sentences.

Take the word 'up', for example.

- Where is the **up** escalator (adjective)?
- We all have our ups and downs and just now I'm enjoying an **up** (noun).
- The village is **up** there (preposition).
- I often walk **up** steps because it is good exercise (adverb).

See what you can do with break, fast, as, set, down – and/or make your own list.

Then try explaining what you've done to someone who doesn't quite understand it. As any teacher will tell you, the best way of really making sure you have grasped something is to teach it to someone else.

7.2 Punctuation

This is a summary of the most important uses of the main punctuation marks used in English. You should revise these fully.

Full stops and other ways of ending a sentence

Make sure you understand the following ways of ending a sentence.

End with a full stop

End every sentence with a full stop (.) Or, if appropriate, use a question mark (?) or exclamation mark (!) both of which include a full stop.

Do not end a sentence with a comma. Remember that some sentences can be very short and short sentences often make for good writing.

Study these two short extracts from Ernest Hemingway's short story *Indian Camp* for correct use of the full stop as a sentence ending. Notice how short some of the sentences are:

> *The two boats started off in the dark. Nick heard the oar-locks of the other boat quite a long way ahead of them in the mist. The Indians rowed with short choppy strokes. Nick lay back with his father's arm around him. It was cold on the water.*
>
> ...
>
> *Across the bay they found the other boat beached. Uncle George was smoking a cigar in the dark. The young Indian pulled the boat way up the beach. Uncle George gave both the Indians cigars.*

Use question marks correctly

Use a question mark if a question is being asked. For example: 'How far is it to York?' 'Are we nearly there?'

Use exclamation marks correctly

Use an exclamation mark if you want to turn something you've written into a joke or to make an exclamation dramatic. For example: 'Help!' 'O my goodness!'

Generally it is bad style, and very lazy, to use exclamation marks other than very occasionally. If your choice of words is strong enough, exclamation marks are usually unnecessary. Think how rarely you see them in newspapers, information books or in good novels (except sometimes in dialogue).

Commas

Commas are used inside sentences. Their job is to make meaning clear. They mark a natural break in the sentence or they separate a part of it from another part. For example:

- Abdul, bring me your homework.
- Put that parcel over there, please.
- A tall man, Mr Smith pulled the book from the top shelf.

They are used to separate items in a list within a sentence. For example:

- Dogs, cats, guinea pigs, hamsters and rabbits all make good pets.
- I've read three books by Dickens, two by Jane Austen, two by Elizabeth Gaskell and one by Thomas Hardy.
- Excited, nervous, exhilarated and passionate, she burst through the door.

Commas are also used in pairs to separate an aside from the main thrust of the sentence. For example:

- It is unlikely, however, to happen.
- Nick Wilkins, a professor of English, told the group about studying the subject at university.
- Adela, who is new to our school, is outstanding at maths.

Capital (or upper case) letters.

Every sentence should begin with a capital letter.

Sometimes handwriting makes it difficult to tell whether a letter is lower or upper case (small or capital). Make sure your writing is not guilty of this. Get out of bad habits if you need to.

Most capital letters are larger than the other letters in a word – make the distinction clearly, especially when the two forms are the same, or similar, shape such as Ss or Kk.

Many are a different shape such as Mm or Dd. Some like Pp and Jj have a different position on the line. Pay attention to this so that the examiner does not think you are misusing capital letters. If it looks to someone who is unfamiliar with your writing as though you are failing to begin sentences and proper nouns with capitals you will lose marks.

You also normally need an upper case or capital letter:

- For names (Estella Jones, Bridgewood Preparatory School, Bristol, River Dee, Tesco and so on). Any proper noun needs a capital letter.
- At the beginning of most lines of poetry (Slowly, silently now the moon / Walks the night in her silver shoon).
- For the first word inside inverted commas (Dick said, 'And I'll come too,' when he saw us getting ready).
- For most initials and acronyms (NATO, RSPCA, GCSE).

Speech marks

Also sometimes called inverted commas or quotation marks (" " or ' ') speech marks always work in pairs. They separate a group of spoken or quoted words from the rest of the sentence.

Note that:

- A capital letter is used each time speech marks are opened unless the speaker is in the middle of a sentence. For example:

  The headmistress said, 'Let us pray.'

  But 'Don't you think,' continued Mary, 'that we should ask permission first?'

- A comma is usually used at the end of the spoken words inside the speech marks before the writer explains who is speaking. For example:

  'Let's go,' said James.

  Or 'That's very interesting,' observed Latifa.

- If a full stop, question mark or exclamation mark comes at the end of a spoken sentence it goes inside the speech marks. For example:

  'Really?' asked Alex

  or 'Wow!' breathed Niamh.

- A new paragraph begins each time a different character speaks.

Study this piece of dialogue as a way of revising speech marks:

> *'Mr Farrow?' he repeated. 'And he, I assume, has sent you to find me for some reason?'*
>
> *'No,' I assured him. 'I have come of my own accord. I am a great admirer of your work, Mr Waring – indeed I am fascinated by it.'*
>
> *He nodded, seeming to accept this as his due.*
>
> *'I have been curious to meet you,' I continued, 'from the first time I set eyes on your Wind carvings.'*

(From *Set in Stone* by Linda Newbery, 2006)

> It doesn't matter whether you use single speech marks (' ') or doubles (" ") but you must be consistent.

If you need to use speech marks within a passage that is in itself in speech marks use the type that you have not already used. This gives one of the following patterns:

> 'Bla bla "bla bla" bla bla.'

or

> "Bla bla 'bla bla' bla bla"

Study this example:

> *'And another thing.' The admiral was still leaning forward. 'Your dossier contains at least one factual error. Clive didn't "surface conveniently installed in my household" … Nash approached me about taking Clive as a replacement, giving him the highest – well "praise" would be more accurate than "endorsement" or "recommendation" … That was twelve years ago.'*

(From *The Secret of the Lost Planet* by Mel Hogan, 2007)

Apostrophes

Make sure you understand the following rules with regard to apostrophes.

Remember how to use 's'

REMEMBER an s at the end of a word usually shows that it is a plural noun (three towns, four dogs, two sticks, etc.) or that it is part of a verb (he says, she runs, Paul sobs).

None of these needs an apostrophe (').

No apostrophe, for instance, is needed anywhere in a sentence like this:

> All the boys in classes one, two and three enjoy basketball lessons but Jules Atkins insists that he prefers card games.

Eight words in this example end in 's'. None needs an apostrophe.

Don't misuse apostrophes

The apostrophe has two uses. It shows:

- possession;
- that letters have been missed out.

When the possessor is singular the apostrophe goes before the s:

- Bernard's dog is the dog possessed by Bernard (one boy – singular).
- A term's work is the work connected with, or possessed by, the term (one term – singular).

When the possessor noun is plural the apostrophe (usually) goes after the s:

- The girls' changing room is the changing room used, or possessed by, the girls (more than one girl – plural).
- Three years' effort is an effort lasting, or possessed by, three years (more than one year – plural).

Watch out for 'ss'

Take care with words which already end in s or ss in their singular or plural form. Exactly the same rules apply:

- The duchess's dress (singular).
- Three actresses' autographs (plural).
- Brahms's first symphony (singular).
- Mr Watts's class (singular).

Note however that in the case of Jesus, we normally write Jesus'.

Note that plural nouns which do not end in s – such as children and women – behave as if they were singular and take an apostrophe before the s when they are possessive. For example: working men's club, children's games.

The apostrophe may also stand in place of missing letters in contracted words such as:

- wouldn't (would not)
- o'clock (of the clock)
- shan't (shall not)

- C'bury (Canterbury – on road signs)
- it's (it is or it has)

Don't get 'it's' and 'its' wrong

Be particularly careful with **its** (which means **belonging to it**) and **it's** (which means **it is** or **it has**).

Learn this example as part of your revision:

- It's a pity that our classroom has its door so close to the street.

Remember that far more words do NOT need an apostrophe than need one. Do your best to learn how the apostrophe is used and get it right in your exam. But if in doubt leave it out. You will make fewer mistakes that way.

7.3 Grammar

Grammar is a big subject and you will by now have studied the details carefully in your English lessons. This section cannot re-teach you the whole of English grammar in a reduced form!

But here are some important things to remind yourself of and to remember as you revise.

If there are any other points of grammar that you know you are not sure about after you have worked through this section then look at *So you really want to learn English* Book 2 or 3. Or ask a teacher to help you.

Agreement of subject and verb

Every sentence has a subject. It may be one word such as **I** … or **Katie** … . It may be something more complex such as **Mr Patterson, our popular and witty Year 6 teacher,** … . The subject often comes at the beginning of the sentence, but it doesn't have to.

Not far from the subject of any sentence is a verb – the action performed by the subject. The sentence may have other things too, but a subject and a verb are the basic building bricks.

It is important to make sure that your subject and verb agree. A singular subject needs a singular verb. If the subject is plural then, of course, it needs a plural verb.

This is pretty straightforward in sentences such as:

- I danced.
- Katie shouted at the top of her voice.
- Mr Patterson, our popular and witty year 6 teacher, retires this year.

But be careful in sentences like this:

- Ellie and Ollie **are** sister and brother. (Plural subject 'Ellie and Ollie' so not 'is'.)

- The weather, the miserable surroundings and the poor facilities **were** all responsible for our unsuccessful holiday. (Plural subject 'The weather, the miserable surroundings and the poor facilities' so not 'was'.)
- Everyone **is** here. (Singular subject 'everyone' so not 'are'.)

Note that these words are all singular and need singular verbs to agree with them:

anybody
everybody
nobody
anyone
each
everyone
everything
either
neither
none

For example

- **Neither** of the men **was** guilty (not 'were').
- We lost several tennis balls but none **was** found (not 'were').
- **Each** of the twenty quizzes **was** harder than the one before (not 'were').

Take care too with collective nouns. They are singular:

- The Labour Party **is** planning its next election campaign (not 'are').
- The choir **is** waiting for its conductor (not 'are').
- The pride of lions **sleeps** most of the day (not 'sleep').

Clauses and phrases

Clauses and phrases are groups of words within sentences.

A clause has a verb of its own. For example:

- A nurse she **had not seen** before came and sat on the edge of her bed.
- And I knew that one day when I **was** bigger I would become one of the top men.
- We were in a small room which **held** nothing except a large grating in the stone floor.

A clause usually adds extra detail to the main sentence, but if you remove it the sentence should still make sense. Try it with the examples above.

A phrase is two or more words used together in a sentence. It does not include a verb. It can be a word group of almost any shape.

- We followed him through the house until we reached the kitchen.
- They had seen the film earlier that evening.
- Given the choice I like fantasy stories best.
- Simon set out wearing full climbing gear.
- Ladies and gentleman, I have an announcement to make.

Good sentences consist of varying patterns of clauses and phrases woven together.

Ten mistakes to avoid in your English

Work through these – perhaps study one a day for a few minutes. Then tick them off when you've practised and understood them.

1. 'I' and 'me'

Don't confuse 'I' with 'me' when you put it with another person. I is usually the subject in the sentence or clause and me the object (direct or indirect). If in doubt leave the other person out of the sentence for a minute and work out what you would write if you were using the pronoun on its own. So you should write:

- Jonathan and I played cricket. (Think of I played cricket.)
- She gave him and me a telling off. (Think of She gave me a telling off.)
- Goodnight from her and me. (Think of Goodnight from me.)
- My twin sister and I are 12 years old. (Think of I am 12 years old.)

2. 'He' and 'himself'

Avoid using himself or herself, or myself or yourself, as the subject (or part of the subject) of a sentence.

- Sarah and myself have … is ALWAYS wrong ✗

3. Get 'too', 'to' and 'two' right

- I am **too** tall for these trousers (too much of something).
- Alex wanted to come **too** (as well).
- She ate **two** ice creams (number).
- May I have permission **to** go **to** the school office? (all other uses including part of a verb or a preposition).

Learn this sentence to help you remember:

Two boys, **too** curious for their own good, ran **to** the cupboard **to** look inside.

4. 'All right'

Strictly speaking, this is two separate words, 'all' and 'right'. The form alright is often seen, and is similar to the forms altogether and already, but is considered bad form in formal writing.

But learn the difference between all ready/already:

- Are we all ready to go? ('Ready' is an adjective telling you more about 'we'. 'All' is a separate adverb telling you more about 'ready'.)
- He has arrived already. ('Already' is an adverb. Here it means 'in good time'.)

5. Remember that 'thank you' is two words. So is 'a lot'.

6. Be careful with 'less', 'few' and 'fewer'

Less refers to quantity. So you can write 'less salt', 'less rainfall' and 'less hope'. Fewer or few refer to a number. So it should be 'fewer eggs', 'few people', 'few schools'. A quick way of remembering this is that if it's something you can count (eggs, people, houses) it is 'few' or 'fewer'. If you can't count whatever it is use 'less'. (One or two British supermarkets have a notice up saying 'Baskets containing fewer than eight items' – which is correct. Several other supermarkets get this wrong. Watch out for it.)

7. Watch out for 'lie'

Learn that 'to lie' is a verb meaning either to put oneself in a horizontal position or to tell untruths. The past tense for the first meaning is 'lay' (I lay on the grass all day yesterday) or 'have lain' (I have lain on the grass all morning and now it's time for lunch).

On Sundays (if you're lucky) you might enjoy a lie-in – and it is an error to call it anything else.

The untruth sense is easier. The past tense is lied or have lied. For example: I lied to him yesterday because I have always lied to him.

The verb to lay is used when the person carrying out the action (the verb's subject) is doing something to something else (technically known as a transitive verb). So you can lay eggs (if you happen to be a hen), bricks, carpets or tables. The past tense is laid or have laid, as in new-laid eggs or a well-laid table.

Remember we're dealing with three different verbs here. Try not to muddle them.

8. Take care with 'only'

It is important to put the word 'only' in the correct place in a sentence. Getting it wrong (as many people do) changes the meaning. Study these examples:

- Only we saw the play that afternoon. (No one else saw it.)
- We saw only the play that afternoon. (We didn't see anything else.)

- We only saw the play that afternoon. (We didn't, for example, read it or rehearse it.)
- We saw the play only that afternoon. (We had seen it very recently.)

Take care with other adverbs such as 'even', 'always' and 'often' too. 'It seemed strange even to us' does not mean quite the same as 'It even seemed strange to us.'

9. 'Practice' and 'practise'

Practice with a 'c' is a noun:

- I must do some clarinet practice.
- Practice is important if you want to improve your tennis.
- Dr Ahmed's medical practice covered three villages.

Sometimes it becomes an adjective:

- The practice rooms are at the back of the music room.
- The hour before supper is cricket practice time.

Practise with a 's' is a verb:

- I must practise the clarinet.
- Practise your tennis if you want to improve.
- Dr Ahmed practises in three villages.

Use **advice** and **advise** to help you remember this. They are easier because they sound different. Say aloud:

- Here is my advice. (noun)
- We could try the advice centre. (adjective)
- I advise you to apologise. (verb)
- She advised me to come. (verb)

Licence/license and **prophecy/prophesy** follow the same pattern.

Be aware that you may see this 'wrong' in American writing. In American English these words are always spelled with a 'c' even when they are verbs.

10. Watch your subjects

If you use a phrase or a clause before the subject of your sentence take care that it does not clash with the subject:

For example:

- Being a wet day, I stayed indoors. (I am not a wet day! You should write: 'It was a wet day so I stayed indoors' or 'I stayed indoors because it was a wet day.')

- Knowing he was ready to begin assembly John stopped talking and listened to the headmaster. (Who is taking assembly? You should write, for example: 'John stopped talking and listened to the headmaster who was ready to begin assembly.' As a revision exercise practise other ways of expressing this sentence so that it says what it means.)

7.4 Spelling

You will have done a lot of work on spelling during English (and perhaps other) lessons over the years. Now, as you revise, it's just a matter of going over the words you know you are likely to get wrong and memorising them. Once you have really mastered a particular word you are unlikely ever to have a problem with it again. And it usually takes only a minute or two's concentration.

Sometimes someone who knows that he or she can't spell a word just avoids writing it in an exam. That is a rather lazy solution and it limits your vocabulary. It is much better to spend a little time learning any spellings you don't know. It will help you in other subjects as well as English.

> You could work with a partner, testing each other, or you might prefer to work alone. Practise writing them. Don't spell them aloud. That is a different skill (and a bit more difficult for most people). In your exam you will need to write them so concentrate on that. You could arrange the words you need to learn in short lists of five or ten a day.

Here, in alphabetical order, are some of the most commonly misspelled everyday words in English. Aim NOT to get them wrong in your exam. Tick each word off if – or when – you are confident that you can spell it:

absence
access
accommodation
achieve
across
address
advantageous
aerial
analyse
anxious
arctic
argument
association
author
autumn
awkward
beautiful
beginning
benefited
biscuit
business
ceiling
changeable
commit
committed
committee
comparison
conceit
condemn
conscience
conscientious
coolly
deceive
definitely
desirable
despair
development
disappear
disappoint
dissatisfy
eerie
eligible
exaggerate
exceed
except
excessive
exhilaration
forty
fulfil
gauge
grammatical
guard
handkerchief
height
holiday
humorous
humour
immediate
independent
install
instalment
irritable
knowledge
leisure
library
likeable
lovable
maintenance
manageable
Mediterranean
miscellaneous
mischief

mischievous
necessarily
necessary
neighbour
niece
ninety
noticeable
occur
occurring
parallel
possession
procedure
proceed
profession
pursue
queue
receipt
receive
recommend
repetition
restaurant
rhyme
rhythm
ridiculous
secretary
separate
sincerely
solemn
success
thorough
truly
vicious
weird
wholly
wilfully
yacht
yield

Summary

You should now know the following:

1. The different word classes or 'parts of speech'.
2. The main punctuation marks used in English.
3. The main grammar points to revise.
4. The ten key things to avoid.
5. Some of the most commonly misspelled words.

Test yourself

Before finishing, make sure you can answer the following questions. The answers are at the back of the book.

1. What is a noun?
2. What is a verb?
3. What is an adjective?
4. What is an adverb?
5. What is a pronoun?
6. What is a preposition?
7. What is a conjunction?
8. Name the three punctuation marks which can end a sentence?
9. What are speech marks sometimes called?
10. Put the apostrophes in the correct place in this sentence:

    Its a great shame that the tree has lost its leaves as its Dads favourite.

Test yourself answers

Chapter 1

Answers may vary but can include:

1. (a) To send out air through the mouth; the movement of the wind; to hit or strike with a weapon.

   (b) A small pointed missile thrown at a board; to move suddenly.

   (c) An alcoholic drink; the soul of a person; a type of ghost.

   (d) The floor of a ship; a pack of cards.

2. (a) Fury; anger.

   (b) Hit; beat; thump; punch.

   (c) Dark; murky; miserable; depressed.

   (d) Tired; worn out; exhausted.

Chapter 4

1. A metaphor is a comparison of one thing with another by pretending that the thing described really is what it is being compared with.

2. A simile is a comparison of one thing with another which makes it clear that it is a comparison by using the words 'like' or 'as'.

3. Personification is the giving of human qualities and abilities to non-humans.

4. Alliteration is the repetition of the same letter (or sometimes sound) at the beginning of neighbouring words.

5. Assonance is the repetition of the same vowel sound (not necessarily spelt the same way) inside neighbouring words.

Chapter 6

1. Answers may vary slightly:

   (a) Liam stretched and yawned. He got out of bed.
   or
   Liam stretched. He yawned and got out of bed.

   (b) Michelle ran to the newsagent's. She opened the door wide, then gasped as she looked inside.
   or
   Michelle ran to the newsagent's and opened the door wide. She gasped as she looked inside.

2. (a) 'That sounds fantastic!' I shouted with extreme delight.

   (b) It sounded great as she explained the detail of her new plan.

3. (a) They descended the path in succession.

   (b) The young bachelor couldn't wait to meet the girl of his dreams.

Chapter 7

1. A noun is a naming word.
2. A verb is an action/doing or 'being' word.
3. An adjective is a describing word which tells you more about a noun.
4. An adverb is a describing word which tells you more about a verb.
5. A pronoun is a word which replaces a noun.
6. A preposition is a word which tells you about the position of something in relation to something else.
7. A conjunction is a joining word.
8. The three punctuation marks which can end a sentence are a full stop, exclamation mark and question mark.
9. Speech marks are sometimes called inverted commas or quotation marks.
10. It's a great shame that the tree has lost its leaves as it's Dad's favourite.